To Honor
Fallen
Heroes

*How a Small German-American
Village in New York City
Experienced the Great War*

JAMES E. HAAS

Also by the Author

"This Gunner at His Piece"
College Point, New York & The Civil War
With Biographies of the Men Who Served

Conrad Poppenhusen
The Life of a German-American Industrial Pioneer

St. Fidelis Parish in College Point, NY
The First Seventy-Five Years
1856-1931

Cover Credit: Sgt. John Harold Embree; Jeb Embree
Author Photo: Joyce Lorenz

TO HONOR FALLEN HEROES
Copyright © 2017, by James E. Haas

Please direct all inquiries to:
www.jimhaasbooks.com
Email: jehaas@comcast.net

Library of Congress Control Number 2017916035

ISBN (Print Edition): 978-0-97241-393-0
ISBN (eBook Edition): 978-0-97241-394-7

Printed in the United States of America

*For all the men and women of College Point,
and elsewhere who have proudly served their
country in times of war and peace.*

Contents

Preface

College Point is a spit of land, almost like a peninsula, situated on the northern tip of Queens County in New York City. Its total area measures all of 2.3 square miles. It is a tiny enclave. *To Honor Fallen Heroes* is an historical and biographical study of the men from this compact village who rendered valuable service to their country in World War One. More than six hundred fifty served in the Army, the Navy, the Marine Corps and the Merchant Marine. Twenty-eight died.

What gives the book its relatively unique character is that the hamlet was basically German in origin, primarily industrial, and in the late 19th and early 20th centuries, a destination place for large numbers of entertainment-seeking New Yorkers. The book includes an overview of these elements, illustrating how each played its role before, during and, to a limited extent, after the war.

Much has been written about this tragic, and costly event. It was costly in terms of money, but more in terms of men's lives, millions of them lost. Countless books have dissected the geopolitical reasons why it occurred, the weaponry and strategies employed, and the imperfect armistice that brought it to a close; the much-debated armistice that was really a prelude to a greater war to come.

These subjects are woven into a detailed analysis of how College Point and its people weathered movements and events; labor strife, anti-German sentiment, espionage, the influenza epidemic, and a host of other forces that impacted American culture in general, and their lives in particular. Also told in chronological fashion and brief vignettes, are the stories of the twenty-eight men who went willingly to war, and died.

Preliminary research began in 2007. At the time, I was not thinking about writing a book, but was curious as to how my hometown responded. I set out with a list of more than 600 names of men who had served. It was printed in the program booklet for College Point's 1920 Memorial Day Exercises. I contacted the New York State Archives in Albany and was able to procure the Military Service Cards for a large percentage of them. Simultaneously, I was able to contact familial descendants of many men who had served, but it was growing increasingly evident that it would be impossible to tell all of their stories. My first book, *This Gunner At His Piece: College Point, New York & The Civil War*, published in 2002, contained short profiles of the 226 College Point men who took part between 1861 and 1865. Because of the sheer numbers involved, a book on how the village experienced World War One required a sharper focus. The ever-expanding array of tools and resources available on the Internet, made that possible with each passing year, and with each book that followed.

Websites such as Ancestry.com. was the source for census records and ship arrival information, years of birth, death and towns of origin, to name just a few. Most beneficial in terms of my subject, were many digitized World War One records. They included the Military Service Records not found in the New York State Archives, Draft Registration Cards, U.S. Army Transport Service Passenger Lists - 1910-1939, and other data points that enhanced individual stories in unexpected ways.

Extremely valuable were websites providing access to historical newspapers. I relied heavily upon www.fultonhistory.com. Site-founder Tom Tryniski has done researchers and historians a tremendous service by developing his site that provides access to digitized versions of a large number of New York State newspapers. The *Greenpoint Daily Star, Daily Star, Newtown Register* and the *Daily Long Island Farmer* were of particular value to me, as soldiers' and sailors' letters were often included in their coverage of war news. *Flushing Daily Times* articles were accessed via http://news.google.com. Enough cannot be said about ProQuest Historical Newspapers available through many library systems. This site allowed for easy access to the *New York Times, Washington Post, Baltimore Sun,* and a host of other newspapers enabling me to read articles describing events as they were reported, and understood at the time they were unfolding,

The staff at the National Archives and Records Administration in College Park, Maryland assisted me in locating the burial records for the twenty-eight men whose lives are briefly profiled. Each of these files brought information to light that was very helpful. Many contained the individual soldier's identification tag that was buried with him. Knowing the fates of all, the simple act of holding them was especially moving. Reading letters from grieving parents vividly brought home the pain, sorrow and anguish they were experiencing.

For investigating historical events, movements, individuals and subjects pivotal or peripheral, www.google.com offered access to repositories of information unavailable to researchers and historians in any previous generation. I am particularly indebted to the staff of the Severna Park branch of the Anne Arundel County, Maryland, Public Library. Using interlibrary loan, they made it possible for me to read print copies of war-related books printed a century ago.

Assembling data surrounding the lives of the men who died in the course of the war was greatly enhanced by familial descendants. The value of their contributions is measureless. I learned more than I could have ever expected through their generosity, given access to original letters and/or photocopies of certificates, medals and assorted ephemera . My special thanks go to Dorothy Weis, niece of August Bigler. Judy Kerr Fluker, great niece of Louis Doerr, Roy Johnert, great nephew of Louis Doerr, Jeb Embree, nephew of John Harold Embree, Nancy Eck, widow of Robert Eck, nephew of Thomas Fagan, Robert T. and James Eck, great nephews of Thomas Fagan, John Schmermund, great nephew of John B. Endres, Thomas Kraemer, great nephew of Arthur Kraemer, John McCormick, great nephew of Thomas McCormick and grandson of John McCormick, William Anderson, great nephew of James J. Powers, Dennis Stack, ancestral cousin of Edward Stack, and Judi Zimmer, great niece-in-law of Henry Zimmer.

The name of every College Point man and woman whose service record was found appears in list form in *To Honor Fallen Heroes*. Over the course of my research, it was my honor and privilege to correspond with many, and to speak with some of descendants of men who were able to return home. They graciously shared stories and recollections of their ancestor. Teri Geib Neilsen/Niece of Jacob Geib, Pat Parker/Albert Mott Ackermann, Lois Kogut/Edward H. Arne, Dan Weatherford/ William Balzer, Arthur Mergenthaler/Barrett family, Rhonda Staudt/ Beigler family, Joseph Bux/Joseph & Charles Bux, Rosalie Maretksy/ Niece of Benjamin Chodes, Daniel Maher/Dockendorf family, Jacob Stein/Charles S. Dubois, Kurt Albert/Reynolds Elliott, J. Edward Starr/ Embree family, Walt Stradling/Golsner family, Sarah Ruch/Golnser family, David P. Harper/Francis Harper's son, Frank Dillmann/Fred & Henry Dillmann, William G. Hoenig/son of William Hoenig, Richard M. Pope, Susan Kufner/Daughter of William Kalwiss, Bernard Klinger/Son of Leopold Klinger, Howard Kullman/Charles Kullma, Robert D. Maeurer Sr./ Grandson of Herman Maeurer, Lawrence C. Martini/Son of Albert E. Martini, Patricia Mahoney/Herman Nostrand, Patrice Brennan/William J. Posthauer, Jack Kellar/Prostler family, Karen Johnson, Bartholomew Prostler, Lois Giblin/Daughter of Wilfred Quick, Helen Biancani/Herbert Riecker, Jean Johnert Roesch/Daughter-in-law of John Otto Roesch, Donald Ray/Martin Shuart, Clifford Serbin/Alexander Serbinski's and Joseph Weinzettle's nephew, Patricia Simpson/Granddaughter of Fabius "Fred" Simpson, Anne Wendel/Sulzbach family, Carl E. Reid/Bernard Vaas, Joann White/Granddaughter of Richard White, Susan Carlson/ Joseph Wilhelm, Hal Zwicke/Martin Zwicke, Beverlee A. (Zimmermann) Brower/ grandniece of Thomas E. Smart

In ways great and small did the following contribute to the writing of this book: Susan E. Brustmann, Executive Director of the Poppenhusen Institute. All data assembled for this book is in the Institute archives. Anyone seeking information on any of the men and women who served is encourgaged to call or visit the Poppenhusen Institute. Su Johnson Cote, Joyce Lorenz, Erda Koehn Ilse Hoffmann, Robert Lewis, Past-Commander, Post 853, William Johann III, Keith Pendegrass, Donald Kunz, Eben Lehman for his information on the Forestry units, Robert J. Laplander for his on the 306th Infantry, Ric Hedman, webmaster of Pigboats.com, a website for anyone interested in WWI-era submarines and the men who served on them, Jim Gandy, Assistant Librarian and Archivist at the New York State Military Museum, Don H. Tolzmann, German historian, Tim Colton, shipbuilding historian, Nathan Rouse, whose Diary of Nathaniel Rouse, Grandpa's Diary of World War One, is posted on the Internet, http://e.wa/home.mindspring.com/wwdiary/, William McQuade, U. S. Naval Academy Librarian (Ret), Lisa Vaeth, Jewish Federation of Greater Hartford, source for Lashiwer family burial information, and Janis Fowler, Louisville Genealogical Society, who helped me find Eva Lashiwer Kessler in a St. Louis area hospital. Joseph Roman improved the quality of many photographs used, and created the schematic for the Bird's Eye View of College Point.

Three persons merit special appreciation. Stephen L. Harris, author and World War One Historian, James K. Fitzpatrick, history teacher, author, columnist, student of the Great War, and friend since elementary school days, and Mitchell Yockleson, Military historian, author and archivist at the National Archives in College Park, Maryland. Each read the manuscript at various stages; all offered beneficial criticism, and suggestions that helped to shape the final work work.

Above all, I want to thank my wife, Lynne, for the support, encouragement and understanding she has given me throughout the writing of this book, and all the others, over the course of our long marriage. Research and writing is time-consuming, much of it stolen. I've been at this game since our earliest days together; her forbearance borders on saintliness.

1

June 5, 1917

While the *New York Times* reported tornadoes wreaking havoc, death and destruction throughout parts of Missouri and Kansas, June 5, 1917 dawned clear in College Point with temperatures expected to be in the low 70's. It was the day President Woodrow Wilson had designated, "Conscription Day", a Tuesday so important that the New York Stock Exchange did something very much out of the ordinary; it did not open.

Having steered clear of Europe's war for as long as possible, and in light of recent events requiring a response, on the second of April he had asked Congress for a declaration of war against Germany. Four days later it was done. This action led to the president's May 18th signing of the Selective Service Act. But in light of certain realities, America was clearly not prepared to go to war. It had a first-class and thoroughly modern navy, but it's army, approaching 108,000 men, ranked seventeenth in the world. It had no modern equipment heavier than its medium machine guns, and had fought its last major battle during the Civil War. National Guard units from the forty-eight states totaled 132,000 men, essentially a part-time, poorly trained militia. The only first-class American force, the United States Marine Corps, 15,500 strong, was scattered around the world. [1] If America was going to fight in a war taking place in Europe, large numbers of well-trained men would be required. Thus was instituted the nation's first national draft.

Come Registration Day, as June 5th was more commonly called, upwards of ten and a half million men across the country signed up. [2]

Slightly fewer than 600,000 came from New York City, [3] approximately 40,000 from Queens. Local Draft Board 176 registered 3,687 men from the five contiguous coumminities of College Point, Flushing, Whitestone, Beechhurst and Malba. [4] To faciliate the process they had registered at one of five possible sites, public schools, 27, 28 and 29, a meat market, and a barber shop. [5] Doors opened at nine in the morning. Candidates assembled in lines extending out the doors and down the streets. With the declaration of war against Germany having taken place just two months earlier, enthusiasm ran high.

A short form was given each man. At the top of the card was a number written in red ink. Based on the total number of anticipated registrants at each site, it was designated the individual's red serial number. The enrollee was then asked to fill out the form; full name, home address, date and place of birth, age, race, and country of citizenship, occupation and employer, a physical description, (hair and eye color, height, disabilities) along with additional information such as address of nearest relative, dependent relatives, marital status, father's birthplace, or previous exemption from service. He then signed the form and was given his pre-induction physical. All who passed had their names placed on a draft list as certified for military service. Failure to register was a punishable offense that could result in a year's worth of jail time, but College Point had few, if any slackers.

The day went off without a hitch. When all requirements were met, each man was given a copy of the form he had signed, his draft card, and directed to keep it in his possession at all times. The document was probably folded, placed in his wallet and forgotten. Those rejected were told to go home and resume their day-to-day activities. Those who passed were advised similarly, but also told it might take as many as four weeks before they learned who would be drafted.

The red serial numbers were drawn in a lottery held in Washington, D. C. in mid-July. The sequence determined who would be called with those drawn earliest most likely to be among those summoned earliest. Exemptions were possible. If you were the son of a widow dependant on you for support, you could apply. If you were a German alien, you could apply. If you qualified under a list of thirteen possible grounds, you could apply. Proof of the claim would have to be furnished in all cases, and there was still no guaranty you wouldn't be called up. Exemption application forms were provided. [6]

Between Wilson's declararation and the June 5th registration, just over two dozen men decided to enlist in either the Army or National Guard. Three days after the declaration of war, notices urging young men to enlist in the U.S. Navy began to appear in shop windows. It was hoped that signs reading, "Attention Young Men of College Point", and pictures showing scenes of actual life aboard navy vessels around the globe, would attract a record number of recruits. [7] Two weeks later, a meeting was held at the Poppenhusen Institute to spur interest in the Naval Reserve, explaining how it differed from the regular Navy. [8] Before Registration Day rolled around, a dozen men had enlisted in the Navy joining another dozen or so who were already serving aboard ships. The Naval Reserve effort had next to no effect, but by year's end, improvement would be shown.

The majority of those who joined the Navy were sent to the Training Station at Newport, Rhode Island. A small percentage of Naval Reserve enlistees were assigned to the Brooklyn Navy Yard, but most went to the Training Station at Pelham Bay Park in the Bronx. Sheltered on a bay on Long Island Sound, it was one of many established by the government for the education of recruits in the ways of the Navy. Once a picnic ground and part of the New York City park system, it was transformed in 1917 into a training facility that could accommodate five thousand men. In addition to all the necessary housing, with its own post office, guardhouse, Y.M.C.A. and canteen, it was a city unto itself. [9]

By war's end, the total number of enlistees for both the Navy and the Navy Reserve, would increase dramatically. Unlike the Army recruits going off to Camp Upton, these men enjoyed neither large-scale going away parties, nor grand parades. In many instances their departures were simply acknowledged in local newspapers.

Unreported in these statistics was that more than half of the College Point men who would willingly, even enthuusiastically serve their country, had Teutonic blood coursing through their veins. As the months passed, that reality would become more generally known. In the middle of the nineteenth century, the grandfathers of some had immigrated from Germany, come to College Point to work in the village's newly constructed rubber factory, and gone off to fight in the Civil War. When the silk mills opened, others of their grandparents, male and female, were hired. Their parents, and perhaps they themselves, had worked in these same mills, had partied at the village's famed waterfront entertainment venues, and hoisted a stein or a glass of beer at any of its countless saloons and watering holes. The town was famous for them. From its earliest days, College Point was a German enclave situated on a small peninsula in northern Queens, renowned for its gemütlichkeit; a destination point for those seeking, jobs, good housing and good times. By most it was called Little Heidelberg; by others, Little Hamburg. How did all this come to pass?

2

Conrad Poppenhusen

Undated Oval Frame Photograph of Poppenhusen

Robert C. Friedrich Collection

In June 1843, twenty-five year-old Conrad Poppenhusen sailed for New York City from Hamburg, Germany to join Adolph Meyer, the son of his mentor, Heinrich Christian Meyer. They went into the business together manufacturing combs, and corset stays from a diminishing supply of whalebone. The Meyer and Poppenhusen Manufactory of Whalebone was situated on the Brooklyn waterfront across the East River from lower Manhattan. Within a year, Meyer left the company; Poppenhusen got a new partner and began a friendship with Charles Goodyear. In time, he was granted limited sole rights to use Goodyear's vulcanization process in the manufacture of combs from hard rubber. It was from this humble product, and others that followed, that his vast fortune was made, equivalent to well over a hundred million dollars today.

The factory thrived over the ensuing decade. In 1854, with the support of new partner Frederick König, Conrad built a grand manufacturing facility in the tiny village of College Point on the shores of Flushing Bay. It was much celebrated in the local press. Commonly referred to as Strattonport at the time, the area consisted of but a few farms, and even fewer houses. The name College Point was derived from the establishment of St. Paul's College in 1839, to educate men for the Episcopalian ministry. The school was located at the extreme north end of the hamlet; it did not succeed.

The village population had grown from under 100 residents in 1852, to upwards of 2,500 men, women, and children in 1860. They were mostly German, and the majority of them worked at the rubber factory. The hamlet had become a magnet for job-seeking immigrants, many of whom Poppenhusen had personally recruited on voyages to and from the country of his birth.

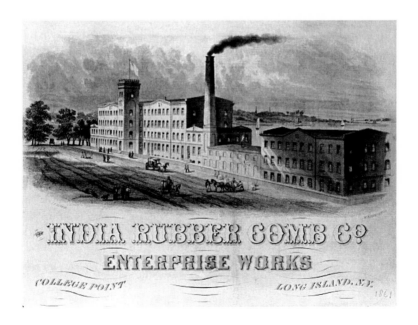

Henceforth, he took it as his charge and mission in life to create a worker's paradise. In doing so, he paved village roads, built houses, deepened and widened the channel of the existing waterway, and served as Justice of the Peace. Poppenhusen also donated a great deal of money to a variety of religious and secular causes. When the American Civil War came in 1861, he paid extra bonuses to his workers, and guaranteed the employment of those who had gone off to fight. He also promised to take care of their widows, and educate their children. It is unlikely that Poppenhusen did not benefit economically from the war, as his company specialized in the manufacture of hard rubber products. While the government had great need for buttons, combs and other accoutrements, demand was great throughout the country. The same held true because of his European contacts around the world.

Three years after Lee surrendered at Appomattox, Conrad established the Poppenhusen Institute. His objective was to provide free education for his workers, and their children. Anyone residing in the area with an interest in learning, was encouraged to take advantage of the offer. Discrimination of any kind, race or creed, was disallowed. Poppenhusen also donated the land on which the mansard-roofed edifice would be placed. He also provided an initial endowment of $100,000. It was followed by a second in the same amount to pay teachers' salaries, and the anticipated long-range cost of operation and upkeep, necessary to continue its celebrated mission of free education. The building opened in May 1870. It included a kindergarten for his employees and the people of the village as well. Unfortunately, a string of failures related to his involvement in consolidating railroads on Long Island, would prevent his from leaving an even greater legacy than he did.

Between 1868 and 1870, he had built stations in College Point and the neighboring village of Whitestone. The railroads he had purchased and consolidated made regularly scheduled stops traveling to and from Manhattan. With a high degree of satisfcation, he departed for Europe with the intention of retiring, but was forced to return many times between 1875 and 1878. Thinking them up to the job, and always available if needed, Poppenhusen had left the running of the rubber factory and the railroads to his sons, Adolph and Herman. Out of touch with what was taking place, he leaned too late they were not up to the task. Hastily returning to America, he was forced to apply for bankruptcy in November 1877, but in less than a year he was able to pay off the totality of his debt. Nevertheless, the vast fortune he had built up over the preceding quarter century was insufficient to make up his losses from the railroads. To all intents and purposes, it was gone.

Poppenhusen went back to Germany, but returned often to College Point. During one fateful visit in 1883, the town founder and philanthropist extraordinaire passed away on December 21st. The *Flushing Journal* was effusive in its praise and description of the funeral arrangements. "The coffin, almost entirely covered with wreaths and immortelles given by the different organizations, was carried into the large hall of the Institute Monday morning, Christmas Eve. The Rev. Mr. Berg of the Dutch Reformed Church officiated at the services and alluded to the benevolence of the deceased, and the good he had done for the community. The funeral procession, about six hundred men, three coaches containing pall bearers, relatives and friends, was formed. It attracted much attention as it passed through the village. The flag was hoisted at half-mast on the liberty pole, the business houses in College Point were closed, and the bells of different churches and factories were tolled as the funeral cortege passed through the village. His remains were taken to Flushing Cemetery, placed in a vault, then shipped in the spring for burial in Hamburg's Ohlsdorf Cemetery.

In the fall of the year following his death, a memorial was erected in a triangular park located near to his elegant mansion home. The granite monument stood twelve feet high surmounted by a bronze bust of the much beloved man. The pedestal on which it rested read:

Poppenhusen
To the Memory of the Benefactor of College Point,
Erected Nov. 1, 1884

3

Silk

B y 1880, College Point's population had risen to 6,000, of which at least 5,000 were German. There were now two large rubber factories, neither of which was owned or operated by the Poppenhusen family. The Goodyear Rubber Company, risen phoenix-like from the ashes of the benefactor's bankruptcy, employed 700 men, women and children. Another venture, called the College Point Rubber Company, employed three hundred.

Almost simultaneously with the onset of Poppenhusen's railroad problems, the silk industry had taken hold in College Point. Hugo Funke arrived in America in 1869. He married Conrad Poppenhusen's daughter Marie, and in 1871, built a silk factory on the shores of Flushing Bay. [1] He called it the Rhenania Silk Works after his beloved Rhine River.

The mill provided jobs to 350 residents and prospered. Profitability made it possible for Funke to enlarge his factory, allowing him to put 150 more people to work. Some had called Conrad Poppenhusen a Benevolent Tycoon, characterizing his attitude toward his employees as caring, verging on paternalistic. Funke, on the other hand, was described as an autocrat, second only to the Czar of Russia. [2] Almost from the start, walk-offs and labor strife plagued him, especially when it came to arbitration. To be fair, Funke was up against challenges Poppenhusen never had to face; the rise of unionism, unending worker demands, increased local competition for business and the need for skilled weavers to work his German-made looms.

Recognizing an opportunity, in 1883 Swiss merchant Samuel Kunz announced plans to erect a new silk factory. His would produce ribbon and be called the Jeanette Silk Works.[3] Soon thereafter, yet a second silk factory opened its doors, and was able to expand in a very short time. German immigrant Jacob Sulzbach purchased ten lots near the railroad station. On it he built a very large factory.[4] In a short time, Sulzbach, a former Funke employee, was able to hire more than 200 people. Rhenania was no longer the only game in town for silk weavers, and persons with usable skills.

Right on the heels of his opening, a third company, Max Hellman & Sons, began operations. This company manufactured low quality, narrow ribbons to compete with Samuel Kunz, who had also opened an ancillary business to dye the product his weavers produced. In time, three additional dye enterprises would move in; Brugger and Wehril, Gerlach & Co. and Rudolph Weber.

Labor issues put Hellman out of business by 1890.[5] Six months later, Sulzbach closed his factory doors saying the action was brought about due to "poor business and general depression in the silk trade."[6] He died in 1897, not living to see two of his grandsons serve during the war. Another company, William Openhym & Sons, began operations. It was incorporated as Myhnepo Ribbon Mills, the name being Openhym spelled backwards.

In the closing decade of the 19th century, the village's silk factory owners and employees were at constant loggerheads. Disagreements between labor and management were unrelenting. They fought over wage increases and salary cuts, working hours and slow downs, stoppages and terminations. They occasionally went out on strike. No company was spared. In 1897, Samuel Kunz retired, and returned to his native Switzerland.[7] The Rhenania Silk Mills shut down in the third week of July 1899. More than 300 were discharged. "Fashion is against us," Hugo Funke said. "In all my thirty years I have never known the condition to be so deplorable."[8] According to some reports, with the shut-down of Rhenania and a strike at Myhnepo Mills, nearly 1,000 men, women, boys and girls had lost their jobs.[9]

The situation did not improve. In the second week of January 1901, the Rhenania Silk Ribbon Mills were sold. A mainstay for thirty years, the mills had provided employment for hundreds of College Point residents. It was now a part of history. A wholesale meat market, it was rumored, would soon occupy the buildings. [10] That did not happen. Instead, the space remained vacant for the next eighteen months. Hugo Funke died in September 1902, [11] and in October the Manhattan Silk Company, a division of William Openhym & Sons, moved its business to the village. [12] Two months later, John W. Rapp, a pioneer in the field of fireproof construction, bought the Rhenania property. He then relocated his United States Metal Products company from Manhattan's Yorkville neighborhood, to the shores of College Point. [13] In the years to come, Rapp's various operations would prove a great success, providing employment to hundreds of village residents. A goodly number would leave their machines in 1917 to go off to war.

In spite of the silk factory troubles, between 1890 and 1900, the village population had risen from 6,100 to 7,000. [14] The increase was fueled by the consolidation of the five boroughs and the ongoing availability of work. Village streets were paved. There was water, gas and two public schools to educate the children. The youngest among them were cared for at the Poppenhusen Institute's free kindergarten. There were three fire companies, a village police force and two newspapers, both published in German. At the north end of the town lived the factory owners and entrepreneurs, their elegant mansions surrounded by lawns and decorative stonewalls. The workers, Germans from all walks of life, lived in the outlying areas, in the many cottages that had been built. There were more under construction. The two groups intermingled somewhat, and their children sat together in the schools. [15]

Real estate values were increasing, as was the demand for waterfront property that could be developed for additional manufacturing purposes. According to some estimates, College Point embraced about four miles of shore or river front. But in addition to being recognized as a rising industrial center second only to Long Island City, College Point was quietly becoming attractive to persons wishing a more bucolic setting. Whereas cows still roamed in fields, Manahttan was easily accessible by ferry or train. Building lots on residential streets could be had for two to five hundred dollars, $13,000 on the high end today. Land along the waterfront, on the rare occasions it became available, was of necessity higher in price. [16] The New York Kerosene Oil Engine Company had the necessary resources. Late in 1901, the company purchased property on 112th Street and 14th Avenue, and there erected a factory to build yachts and working boats. A man named George Stelz was placed in charge. [17] When the war came, a firm he had started, the College Point Boat Company, would be called upon to build small wooden vessels called submarine chasers. Because of their size and speed, they were particularly effective against submarines, Germany's undersea menace. [18]

As the new century dawned, day-to-day life continued in College Point. The village had grown into a very important manufacturing center. At the same time, two popular, large-scale waterfront entertainment venues had transformed College Point into a summertime destination point for those seeking good time, as well as for those seeking political office. One was run by Joseph M. Donnelly, the other by Joseph Witzel.

SAMUEL KUNZ, SILK MILL, MFR. NARROW RIBBONS.

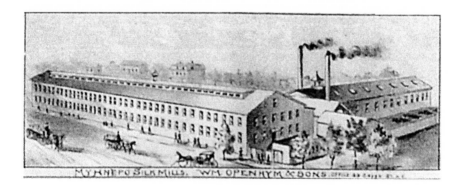

MYRNEPO SILK MILLS, WM. OPENHYM & SONS.

4

Beer, Breweries
and Gemütlichkeit

B efore either of these men impacted the entertainment business in
College Point, there were saloons and breweries. From its earliest
days, the brewer's art was practiced in the village. Bavarian Joseph Thaler
was one of three such artisans present in 1860. By the time the next census was taken, he had died and his widowed wife was running their beer
garden. Not long thereafter, the Thaler family was out of the business
altogether. Large-scale breweries, one after another, made their presence
known offering jobs for those having the requisite skill and experience.

Between 1870 and 1910, a building on 14th Road and 120th Street
was the premier site for brewing beer. One Moritz Levinger got it started
before non-payment of taxes [1] forced him to give way to Messr.'s Hirsch
and Herman. Unable to pay their water bills, the owners sold out to the
Fitzgerald Brewing Company of New York City. [2] Fitzgerald occupied
the premises for only a short time, two years. New management not only
acquired the brewery in 1891, it was given a new name, Mutual. [3] Its product was sold almost exclusively to the village's beer gardens and saloons,[4]
most assuredly a limited market. A substantially increased state liquor
tax created financial difficulties, as did strikes at the plant. Both factors
eventually forced Mutual into receivership. [5] George Karsch purchased
the business in June 1896, [6] but two years thereon, his operation began
to experience labor disputes of its own. As had happened in the village's

silk shops, strikes followed, people lost their jobs and others were hired as replacements. While supported by New York City-based unions, [7] the over-all community considered the action unjustified. [8] A decade-long period of relative calm followed. Then, in mid-July 1910, Karsch sold out to the Central Brewing Company of Manhattan. [9] That decision hastened an end to the forty-year saga of brewing beer in College Point. It had been a long and bumpy ride.

Intimately joined with the brewing industry were the countless beer gardens, summer gardens, hotels and waterfront entertainment venues for which the village was famous. Two goliaths in the latter group gave College Point a cachet that lasted over the same forty years. One was Joseph Witzel's Point View Island, the other Joseph M. Donnelly's Boulevard Hotel, Park, Restaurant and Pavilion. The former was located on an expanse of prop-erty at the northernmost part of the village referred to as Tallman's Island. Its land mass was once separated from the mainland of College Point by tidal marshland, hence its name. The latter occupied an area almost equal in size on the northeast and northwest sides of 115th Street at 14th Road.

Joseph Witzel, a recent German immigrant, was twenty-four years old in 1860, and one of College Point's few young men who did not see service during the Civil War. Recently married, he worked as a shoemaker as he would for the next decade.

On July 4, 1871, two years after he had brought it to the village, Conrad Poppenhusen's Flushing and North Shore Railroad ran sixty-seven trains into College Point. They carried 20,000 passengers. 15,000 of them got off at the station for the singular purpose of spending the day celebrating the holiday. Area beaches were filled to capacity, and the beer gardens were jammed. When darkness fell, a huge fireworks display lit up the nighttime sky. [10]

Anticipating the future, in that same year Joseph Witzel purchased a piece of property on the corner of 119th Street and 14th Road on which he built a small hotel. Later, he purchased surrounding property, and there erected a large pavilion and dance hall. [11] It soon became a very popular watering hole. With Donnelly's place situated just one block north and five to the west, Witzel could not help but notice how much his competitor's catering business had grown in what was really a very short time. Nor could he miss seeing how much the crowds enjoyed the Irishman's clambakes and chowder parties.

In October 1883, residents came out to watch a parade in celebration of the 200th anniversary of the advent of Germans coming to America. Cadres of young men stepped off to the marching pace set by two drummers. Large crowds of spectators lined each and every street cheering as columns of boys bearing arms, dressed in cadet gray or blue and wearing slouch hats, passed by. American and German flags flew in the wind. White geese that filled the paved roadways parted like whitecaps in front of a vessel's prow as the parade made its way to Donnelly's woods. Several kegs of beer were unceremoniously opened. Speeches in German and in English [12] were followed by athletic contests and choral singing provided by four of the village's renowned musical societies, the *Harmonie, Liedrekranz, Alpenroesli* and *Saengerlust*. [13] At nightfall the pavilion was brilliantly illuminated; fireworks lit up the grove. Young men and women flocked to the place to dance and frolic late into the evening. [14] The little village of College Point was flourishing, and nine out of ten people living there were German. Joseph Donnelly was an exception. Born in Brooklyn in 1842, his roots lay in Ireland.

Donnelly began his career working as an agent for New York City's George Ehret's Brewery. He imported other lagers in the late 1870's, and even bottled beer in the village under his own trademarked name.[15] Operating his popular venue since at least 1876, it was only in early February 1892 that he was able to purchase the hotel and grove property. He paid $45,000 for it,[16] more than $1,000,000 today.

In this same year Joseph Witzel seized on an opportunity to purchase Point View Island. It had been a successful waterfront venue in business for a decade. Operated by John H. Starin, a former Republican Congressman from upstate New York, he had previously converted a number of islands in Westchester County on Long Island Sound into a summer resort for city dwellers. He called it Glen Island. Because he also owned the Starin City River & Harbor Transportation Company, it was his steamships that transported thousands of visitors to the venue. It featured a German beer garden, a bathing beach, a railway and even a Chinese pagoda. By 1882 attendance had reached 500,000, and within six years it broke a 1,000,000.[17]

With the success of his resort in Westchester County, Starin sought out additional opportunities. In 1882 he leased the Point View Island property. A 400-foot long dock was built onto which his excursion steamers could deliver their crowds of weekend and holiday merrymakers. The extensive grounds were beautifully landscaped with bridle paths. Lanes and winding walks were especially inviting to young couples that wished to be alone. There was also a huge dining room, and four baseball diamonds for inter-company and inter-club contests. Starin hired Joseph M. Donnelly to be his site manager. It was a position he would leave in 1887 in order to return to managing his own facility.[18]

Witzel took over the Starin lease when the site became available in 1892. Sooner or later, everyone seeking or holding office came to College Point, the more successful on an annual basis. They traveled by ferryboat and steamboat; they arrived on trolleys and trams and eventually automobiles, Democrats and Republicans alike. Senators shook hands, Mayors kissed babies, congressmen and aldermen answered questions. Career politicians all, it would seem, solicited votes. Even Teddy Roosevelt made it a point to get to the "Point." That's where the people were. As they gleefully exited the watercraft or land conveyance upon which they arrived, either Witzel at Point View, or Donnelly at his Grove, would welcome thousands of revelers on a daily, and non-stop basis. The season ran from Decoration Day, as May 30th was called, through late fall. The partiers came from all walks of life; individuals, entire families, countless groups and organizations al looking forward to a day of food, fun, and frolic in these two shrines to enjoyment. Both were referred to by many as Mecca.

Two thirds of College Point's perimeter was and remains shoreline, but the Donnelly and Witzel operations were far and away the prime locations. High or low tide, the water was deep enough to allow the big steamers to tie up at the respective piers, and remain there through the day. Indeed, summer gardens and saloons were ubiquitous, the village's stock and trade. They were owned and operated by men with names that could have been taken directly from a Hamburg telephone directory; Freygang and Angenbroich, Steiner and Winterstoefer, Zehden, Weber, Bunge, Dietz, Alsheimer, Hildebrandt and Muhlenbrink to name just a few. One or two Irishmen, or at least men with Irish surnames, were also in the lager dispensing business. Civil War veteran Thomas Egan was one; James Deakin another. Both were definitely in the minority. All of these names appeared on an 1896 bird's eye view lithograph of College Point, but none of them held a candle to Donnelly or Witzel.

Both men offered the same standard program. Massive breakfasts served with grace and efficiency would commence as soon as arrivals could be corralled into the large dining halls. If the weather was agreeable, athletic contests of all sorts followed; bowling and baseball games, 100, 220 and 440-yard dashes, thin man, fat man and three-legged races, and the occasional shooting contest. For those who wished a more casual pace, rowboats were available as was swimming. All in all it was a perfectly glorious way to spend an afternoon, with time for a nap before dinner that began promptly at six.

Though competitive in business, the two Josephs were also fiercely devoted to their church, St. Fidelis, and its pastor Ambrose Schumack. Both had known his predecessor, Joseph Huber, who had started the congregation in 1856. Witzel had been numbered among his first parishioners. Huber died on New Year's Eve 1889 with Schumack arriving a day or two earlier. While the College Point Catholic Church had never benefited specifically from the beneficence of Conrad Poppenhusen, the two entrepreneurs made up for the oversight, outdoing each other in terms of generosity.

When a new church building was dedicated in 1895, both men were serving as parish trustees. Their names were memorialized on stained glass windows each had donated. There were other gifts as well. In October 1906 on the occasion of the parish's fiftieth anniversary, Witzel donated the church bell, and a gift of $1,500. At the same time, Donnelly funded a new altar along with $1,000. [19] Two months later, and two days before Christmas, Joseph M. Donnelly passed away. He had been ill for some time. [20]

Within four years, two of his sons, neither having reached the age of thirty, also died. A third son, his namesake, took over the family business, but it struggled. By late 1916 Joseph Donnelly Jr. leased the 14-acre grove and its pavilions to a stage and silent film actor seeking to have his own movie production company. [21] It was yet another fledgling industry setting up shop in College Point, but it would not be successful.

Witzel succumbed to a heart attack in October 1913. His Point View Island, fondly remembered for its political gatherings, church picnics and athletic events, was sold in the fall of 1925. At the time it was presumed that private homes would be built on the twenty-four acre tract of waterfront land. [22] Instead, in order to process the large amounts of effluent expected as a result of the 1939 World's Fair, the City of New York transformed it into the Tallman's Island Sewage Treatment plant. But that was long in the future.

5

1900 - 1913

Around the turn of the 20th Century, teaching the German language in public schools was under attack as part of the overall question of the German people's assimilation into the greater American culture. [1] Teaching the language in village schools had a been a precedent since the day Conrad Poppenhusen opened his Institute's doors, paying the teacher's salary out of his own pocket. College Pointers had debated this same question in 1885 along with the practice of reciting the Lord's Prayer at the start of each school day. Both measures passed. [2]

Sixteen years later, the community was again debating the same issues and thoroughly displeased that the questions had not been resolved once and for all. Townspeople raised their voices in protest just as loudly as had their forebears. Many of the village's Irish, able to read and write the language passably, agreed, holding to the collective belief that since College Point was first inhabited by German, it was their right as taxpayers to demand that the German language be taught in their schools. Despite arguments presented, and protests raised, the language was removed from the curriculm. Thirteen months later it was reinstated. [3] Prayers before class of any kind remained an open issue.

Bias was not confined solely to what language could be taught. There were also signs of prejudice against women. The village's new school, P.S. 27, had opened in 1899. Among its offerings was a training school for adult foreigners. Classes were held in the evening, but due to a Board of Education rule, men and women were not permitted to receive instruction in the same building. [4] Fifty-two pupils were set to begin classes in 1902, but twenty-six women who had applied were turned away, even though there was more than enough room to accommodate both sexes. [5] The issue was eventually resolved, the school had a successful opening night, and adults of both sexes received instruction together in English; the language of their new land.

Ethnicity and assimilation were widespread subjects during this time period, especially with regard to Germans. St. Fidelis pastor Ambrose Schumack had labored tirelessly on behalf of German and Austrian immigrants, and was well recognized for his efforts at home and abroad. [6] August Ebendick, since 1864 pastor of the village's St. John's Lutheran Church, continued to preach in German through 1910. Seeing the signs of the times, he had also established the English Church of the Holy Spirit for those who preferred the church's liturgy in English. [7] Rev. John Baumeister's First Reformed Church had a largely German congregation, but its transformation was also in progress as the children and grandchildren of original settlers became more and more Americanized.

Other predictable changes were underway. Many of the village's original residents and leaders had either already died or were in the declining years of life. Existing factories continued to expand one among among them the Issac B. Kleinert Rubber Company. It had been in operation since 1886. His enterprise grew fairly rapidly the result of one internationally known item, dress shields for women's clothing. An expanded product line included shower and bathing caps, baby pants and rubber sheeting material. While there are no monuments to Kleinert in College Point, from the day he opened his factory he gave employment to multiple generations of people, including a number who went to war in 1917; and one who gave his life.

Another was John W. Rapp. He enjoyed national fame in the building trades by his work in originating bronze and steel trim, and metal doors that made otherwise dangerous structures, absolutely fireproof. Rapp had brought his factory, one of the largest of its kind in the United States, from Manhattan's Yorktown neighborhood to College Point in 1902. In years to come, many skyscrapers prominent in the New York City skyline would be safer using his products. The Metropolitan Life Insurance Company, the Woolworth Building, and the Manhattan Municipal Building at One Centre Street, along with many other skyscrapers in the larger cities across the country, were made safer. Rapp became a very wealthy man as a result.

In the final years leading up to 1914, a good number of new manufacturing enterprises opened their doors providing more employment opportunities. The large rubber factories continued to expand, and some silk mills were still in operation. Following on the heated discussions that had taken place around the turn of the century, the incidence of referring to College Point as a thoroughly German village, or setting it apart as anything other than a good site for manufacturing, or for making one's home, decreased. More important to its everyday life were the concerns present in all communities. They included good governance, continued improvement of infrastructure and services, expansion of employment opportunities and maintenance of the quality of life it had enjoyed for more than fifty years. With the majority of the homes in College Point either actually or destined to be single-family units, its small town character was preserved, and its population growth very likely to be manageable for some time to come.

There was no denial of its German character; there was simply no emphasis on it. The *Brooklyn Daily Eagle* ran a regular feature headlined "In German Circles." When College Point was mentioned, it was more often than not to highlight an event at Point View Island or Donnelly's Grove attended or sponsored by a German society or church group. At other times a concert by the village *Maennerchor* or other German musical event might be publicized or, in one case, a list of the new officers elected by the newly established motorcycle club whose names happened to be German. Appearing with greater frequency were stories about the village's roads, factory openings, and expansions; its real estate sales, church announcements, and sports teams, not to mention countless promotions of political events.

Queens was growing steadily, with College Point very much a part of the story. The common belief that people born there and grown to maturity spoke only German, and unable to understand English, was by this time, far-fetched. One source said that the population was fifty percent German or had German ancestry, but that estimate was low; it was much higher. With good housing, good churches, good schools, lots of jobs and an active love for their country adopted or otherwise, College Point's German populace were by and large, just good citizens. When the war came, the young men of the village gave a willing and resounding response to the nation's call to arms; some gave their all.

St. Fidelis Roman Catholic Church

St. John's Evangelical Lutheran Church

St. Paul's Episcopal Church

First Reformed Church

Rev. Ambrose Schumack

Rev. August Ebendick
St. John's Church Archives

Rev. Benjamin Mottram

Rev. Arthur Halfmann

Rev. Henry Sluyter
First Reformed Church Archives

6

1914 - 1916

As 1914 unfolded, the powers of Europe were seemingly at peace. Ships from Germany, Austria, Russia, England and France traveled freely on the high seas. International commerce was booming, and it appeared civilization had finally achieved the beginnings of perpetual peace. The illusion was temporary.

The Balkan States and Greece had made war on Turkey in 1912, been successful, and divided the spoils. German powers intervened and let the Balkans know they were to be ruled by Austria. This did not sit too well with the Russians, and they did not plan to sit idly by.

France still lamented the loss of Alsace-Lorraine during the Franco-Prussian war. It had started on July 19, 1870, and ended the following May 10, 1871. At the commencement of fighting, the Germans in College Point organized a society for the purpose of forwarding money to support the soldiers and comfort the wounded. A substantial amount was raised. [1] When the war ended, the village held a German Peace celebration. Two thousand persons marched through the streets, the long procession terminating at Donnelly's Grove. Here everyone enjoyed large and copious drafts of German lager and Rhine wine, while listening to a band play the *"Poppenhusen March"* composed in honor of the town's benefactor. [2] If there were any French émigrés living within its boundaries, it is unlikely they took part in the festivities. Forty-three years later, if the opportunity to recover their lost territory presented itself, few French citizens would think twice about the possibility.

England had anxiety over Germany's expanded maritime capability, and the potential challenge it posed to her naval power. She was, after all, the long-time mistress of the seas. As far as Germany and Austria were concerned, a month after Crown Prince the Archduke Franz Ferdinand's June 28th assassination in Sarajevo, the Austrian government essentially told Serbia they were taking over, and declared war. Russia was not pleased. Then Germany declared war on Russia. England suggested a conference with Germany, Italy and France. Germany responded saying they would do nothing to prevent Russia and Serbia from suffering final subjugation, or war. Germany declared war on France. Great Britain declared war on Germany. Poor little Luxembourg and Belgium. Though long-time neutrals, both were soon overrun by the German army. Declarations of war, country against country, continued. Within a week of the assassination, the great European struggle that came to be called World War One had begun.

Many travelers were stranded in Europe. Thought to be on vacation in Austria, St. Fidelis pastor Ambrose Schumack was acutally undergoing surgery for an unspecified illness. John H. Gerlach was in Germany on business. His loose-leaf book binding factory employed many of College Point's young men. Bakery owner George Krell and his wife were touring the continent with plans to visit her family in Denmark. [3] The outbreak of war delayed their return, but all made it home safely to the relief of parishoners, friends and family.

With war such a new reality, it can only be surmised that College Point's sympathies mirrored those of many German-American New Yorkers who supported the Fatherland. It was accepted belief that were Germany to defeat France, the next battles would be fought against the English. [4] There were some Irish-Americans strongly supportive of Germany over England, but their fight was more with the latter than the former. Since many College Point's families were made up individuals from both heritages, strain was inevitably present. Thinking themselves more as Americans, and less as members of a specific ethnic group, villagers persevered. So too did others in similar situations across the county. In a Thanksgiving Day *New Yorker Staats-Zeitung* editorial, Herman Ridder wrote, "We are a people mixed in blood, but in mind we are one… Americans in the highest, noblest and most sacred sense of the word." [5]

Some areas of the United States regarded German-American immigrants as second-class, but such was probably not the case in College Point. In the early months of the war, those with Teuton ancestry were very likely not passionately pro-German, though it is equally safe to say they probably wanted Germany to win. Had America been attacked, most would have considered it a duty to volunteer. A small portion however, would have probably refused to fight, even if drafted. An infinitesimal number might have given aid and comfort to the enemy, though nothing of the sort made the papers.

It is also quite possible that many College Point families with German roots had cut most ties to Europe. For some, their once native tongue had become almost a foreign language. Some considered the conflict in Europe a family war, in that the British, Russian and German monarchs were cousins. The same could be said of many families in College Point. An unknown number could have easily had relatives; brothers, cousins or uncles fighting on the front lines.

To be sure, a number of residents would have had awareness that feuds between the countries of Europe had been going on for ages, simultaneously hoping that America would stay out of it. President Wilson's lean toward neutrality seemed to indicate such would be the case. Typically, residents' primary concerns would have been with their own affairs. Like many Americans and with a few exceptions, they lacked interest in, and knowledge of, European history, geography and politics, and doubtless hoped that the storm clouds would blow over. A war with Germany was something unthinkable.

In mid-March 1915, as millions of soldiers wallowed in the trenches of Europe, slaughtering or being slaughtered, College Point's *Maennerchor* played host to the showing of "a fine collection of German war pictures at the recently opened Lyceum Theater. The big playhouse was jammed, and the German soldiers on the screen were greeted with storms of applause. Three shows were given, and each time the house was sold out." [6]

College Pointers were shocked to learn that Mrs. Katherine Dingley had been one of the passengers reported missing on board the *Lusitania* sunk by a German U-boat on May 7th. The Dingley's were well-known in the town, as her husband Howard, whose actual name was Edward, had worked as a foreman for John W. Rapp. Mrs. Dingley was traveling to England to join her husband who had left on an earlier ship. [7] Unknown to all who sailed on the vessel, but widely reported in the press, almost all the *Lusitania's* hidden cargo consisted of munitions and contraband destined for the British war effort. Newspapers across the country called the sinking an act of war. Over one thousand passengers were lost, one hundred of them Americans. President Wilson protested strongly to the German government. Its response was merely to say that unrestricted submarine warfare would continue, resulting in the loss of more American lives. Beyond Wilson's protestations, the United States did nothing formal by way of response.

When compared to Britain's blockade of food to non-combatants in Germany, those who followed the war closely might not have considered the action sufficient reason to get involved, no matter the cost in human life. Similarly, they were probably not all that ready to absolve Germany of all guilt finding no defense in her invasion of Belgium. All was not cut and dried, nothing was set in stone; none of the Allies, England, France and Russia were lily-white.

In mid-June, it was reported that John W. Rapp had refused two large orders from an American firm for munitions amounting to more than a million dollars. He had received orders for gun barrels, and shrapnel shells at the beginning of the war, but declined to fill them. "I refuse to make anything that is destructive, and I refuse to participate in the slaughter of so many men in Europe by the things manufactured here. Born in New York City to an Irish mother and an Alsatian father, he went on to say he would refuse orders for the Teuton allies, as well as their enemies."[8] America was not as yet a participant; the situation would change in less than a year.

With German zeppelins bombing Paris, and German submarines continuing their campaign of piracy and pillage, the Battle of Verdun began in early February 1916. Together with July's Battle of the Somme, it would bring about the loss of more than a million lives; 400,000 British, 200,000 French and 450,000 Germans. On April 24th, Easter Monday, Ireland's rebellion had its start in Dublin coming to its conclusion on May 30th, but not really putting an end to the troubles. As with abandon, countries across Europe continued to declare war on one another, resulting in countless combatants being slaughtered in trenches on all sides.

Come April, the New York City Plan Commission issued a report on the location of industry in Queens. [9] A subsequent study produced by the Long Island Railroad determined that College Point was the home of eighty-eight factories, employing more than 3,250 people. It was second only to Long Island City, far ahead in the total number with 738 of the former, and more than 18,000 people employed. Queens had a greater number of employees in its factories than any other county in New York State. [10]

A number of large enterprises had relocated to College Point, one of the largest being the British-American Chemical Company based in England. Embargoes imposed on the importation of pharmaceuticals and other chemistry-related products, made it necessary to begin producing its wares on this side of the Atlantic. Operations were soon underway in a vacant John W. Rapp-owned building on 15th Avenue and 117th Street. It was expected the company would hire a large force of men. [11] At the very same time, the National Chain Company, a Manhattan-based firm, leased space, and was expected to hire many men. [12] With the prospect of war growing more and more likely, and the probable increase in demand for its products, the American Hard Rubber Company submitted plans to erect another three-story factory building. [13]

Notably, a firm called L.W.F. Engineering, one of a handful of companies in the United States on the cutting edge of aviation technology, had recently moved its Long Island City operation to College Point. [14] There was a double meaning to its three-letter name. On the one hand, each was the first letter in the surnames of the three founding partners; Edward G. Lowe, Charles F. Willard and Robert G. Fowler. All were aviation pioneers in their own right. On the other hand, the letters were symbolic of one of the main features of the planes they produced; a laminated wood fuselage. College Point was a natural choice soon after the trio recognized the need for larger quarters fit for expansion, with water access. Leasing a large parcel of waterfront land in July, the company planned to build aeroplanes. [15]

Long Island City and College Point, the two leading manufacturing centers in the borough, found it increasingly difficult to secure enough employees. For those involved in manufacturing, almost any form of manufacturing, the axiom was true; war made for good business, good business indeed. [16]

As the last quarter of 1916 began, L.W. F. Engineering was awarded a U.S. Navy contract to build six *aeroplanes* and motors [17] in addition to aircraft ordered just prior to the company's relocation. [18] There were more orders yet to come.

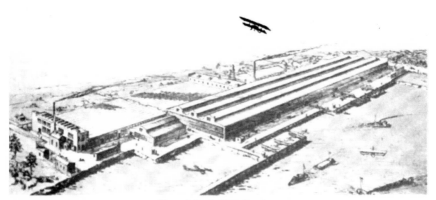

Plan of the L-W-F Plant

7

Call to War

On January 16, 1917, Johann von Bernstoff, German Ambassador in Washington, received a coded telegram from Arthur Zimmermann, Foreign Secretary to the German Empire in Berlin. Its contents were to be forwarded to the German ambassador in Mexico City. Intercepted, and decoded by British Naval Intelligence cryptographers, it was learned the German government intended to resume unrestricted submarine warfare. This was a policy it had suspended due to strong American protests after the Lusitania sinking. Any merchants ship found in international waters would be sunk without warning. Heretofore, German boats, surface or submarine, had been required to stop such ships, allow the crew to take to the boats, provide them with food and water and assist their passage to the nearest landfall. When this was done, the vessel could then be destroyed. The German high command feared the unrestricted policy might draw America, to this point in time neutral, into the conflict. Nevertheless, it was scheduled to go into effect on the first day of February. [1] This action placed the issue of war or peace squarely before the United States.

The telegram instructed the German Ambassador that in the event the U.S. appeared likely to enter the war, he was to approach the Mexican Government with a proposal to enter an alliance. Germany would offer aid to Mexico in the reclamation of territory lost during the Mexican-American War of 1848 and the Gadsden Purchase, specifically the American states of Texas, New Mexico and Arizona. Bernstoff was further charged to urge Mexico to help broker an alliance between Germany and the Japanese Empire. In an effort to protect their intelligence from detection, and to capitalize on growing anti-German sentiment in the United States, the British waited until February 24th to present the telegram to Woodrow Wilson. A week later on March 1st, the story appeared in newspapers across America.

Mexico declined the proposal, but upon learning what the German government had attempted to do, the American people, a large proportion of them German, were outraged. [2] Simultaneously, the country grew less and less neutral, more settled in acceptance of the likelihood that war was on the horizon.

College Pointers went on about their normal activities. German bakers awakened early, lit their ovens, and prepared the numerous confections, breads, and rolls they hoped to sell. At the same time, Samuel Pores a Jewish butcher whose two sons, Daniel and Charles were nationally recognized New York City roadrunners, opened his doors. So too did other local Jewish merchants Celie Gessner, her millinery shop, David Leppel, his dry goods store, and Philip Wolinksy, his law office. College Point had a small yet growing Jewish community made up of merchants, and professionals, but it was also home to workers of many nationalities. As the eight o'clock whistles blew, men and women, the more settled Germans, Swiss, and Irish along with their most recently arrived neighbors, Hungarians, Danes, and Italians, passed through the doors of the village's many factories, and set about together doing the day's work.

At this time, College Point was not so much a village defined by neighborhoods segregated by ethnicity. Rather, identity came about through other determinants such as the section of the town a person lived in, the church or school attended or perhaps the social groups or organizations joined. It was once demonstrated that this tiny enclave had more societies, lodges and clubs than any other village of its size in the State of New York. [3] There was little or no Black presence, that population having reached its zenith in pre-Civil War days. Subsequent censuses taken every ten years showed a continual decline in this segment of the village's population. When the 1915 census was taken it was virtually non-existent. [4]

Inadvertently, or perhaps by design, College Point's residents lived and worked closely together. At the same time, they retained their individuality because over the decades the village trustees had not approved the erection of any tenement style housing. As a result, home ownership was pretty much the norm. Institutions, such as the churches, served five separate denominations, and the growing Jewish community, by its very nature, fostered a degree of separateness and autonomy. On the other hand, membership in, and affiliation with other social, political and business groups, brought the population very close together on many occasions, and in numerous capacities.

German submarines sunk seven steamships in the first quarter of the year. On March 18th, newspapers reported three vessels flying the American flag had gone to the bottom. The steamer *Vigilancia* was torpedoed without warning. *City of Memphis*, the second ship, was shelled and then torpedoed after the crew had been given fifteen minutes to take to the lifeboats. All survived. The *Illinois* was reported merely as having been sunk. Again there were no casualties. [5]

As a result of this report, and others, the worst fears of the German high command were realized. On April 2nd President Wilson asked Congress for a declaration of war. Congress responded four days later, authorizing and directing the entire naval and military forces of the United States, and the resources of the Government, to carry on war against the Imperial German Government to a successful termination, using all the country's resources.

Almost immediately, more than 1,700 German and Austrian seamen, whose ships happened to be berthed at New York Harbor piers, were rounded up and taken to Ellis Island. Everyone, officers and crewmen alike, were denied their ration of beer, and told the summer sea breezes would be very invigorating. "There was no truth that they were being treated as prisoners," said the Commissioner of Immigration." "No one had yet complained. The food supply was equally good and adequate, and the health of all was being watched over by health officers." [6]

Articles in support of the war filled the pages of the nation's newspapers. Austrian-born Father Ambrose Schumack told his mostly

German-American congregation, "their first duty was to America, and that they must give undivided allegiance to the government." [7] German organizations, societies and clubs across the country were loud in their protestations and proclamations of loyalty. On the one hand, men with Teuton blood coursing through their veins were being encouraged to enlist. [8] On the other, movements were afoot to bar un-naturalized Germans, regardless of how long they had been living in the country, from passing through, working in, or doing business within a half mile of restricted armory zones. One of these was George Stelz's College Point Boat Company; another L.W.F. Engineering Company. It was declared a zone unto itself. [9]

The third weekend in May was of particular consequence for the nation, for New York City and for College Point. President Wilson signed the Selective Service Act designating June 5th as Registration Day for men between the ages 21 and 31. Two weeks later, alien Germans, be they butchers, bakers, waiters whatever, living in or near to armory zones, had to appear before the United States Marshal in Manhattan. All had to file an application for a permit, and then swear an oath of allegiance. [10] With so many factories in New York City gearing up for war work, and especially in Queens, the Marshal's office was overrun. More than five hundred German aliens waited in line to do as directed. Within ten days, more than 45,000 German citizens living within the five boroughs, had submitted applications. United States Marshall Thomas McCarthy, expressed astonishment. [11]

Over this same weekend, newspapers reported the awarding of Navy contracts for the construction of eighty-nine submarine chasers designed to seek out and do battle with the undersea enemy. The College Point Boat Company received an order to build ten in 110 days. Specifications called for them to be made of wood, be fifty to sixty feet long, and capable of reaching speeds in excess of forty miles per hour. The government would supply the 750 horsepower motors, along with high-powered rifles and rapid-fire machine guns to be mounted one each, fore and aft.

The ocean-going boats were to be delivered, fully equipped and sea-worthy, within the specified time frame. Stelz's men, presently hard at work launching pleasure boats, were soon laboring day and night on their new project. They would shortly be joined by a large number of skilled mechanics, as many as George Stelz could get. [12] An armed guard was put on duty to protect the company as part of the village's armory zone, [13] and before long, additional College Point manufacturers and factory owners received governement orders for war materials.

As June 5th drew to a close, the community had gone on about its normal routine. Such was not the case for one thousand-plus men born between 1886 and 1896. They had spent at least part of their day registering for the draft, being examined, prodded and poked. Those who passed muster were told to go home and wait.

Twenty-two year-old Charles A. Kullman, a first-generation German, would spend an uneventful summer driving a truck for a local ice dealer. But three months later, almost to the day, he would become the village's first draftee to be ordered to Camp Upton. [14] Ironically, Kullman would serve one of the shortest tours of all College Point inductees. In mid-December, he would be honorably discharged on a non-specific Surgeon's Certificate of Disability, and sent home. [15]

By the end of the year upwards of 250 College Point men would be serving in all branches of the armed forces, the Army, Navy and Marine Corps. [16] They were just the tip of the iceberg.

8

Camp Upton and Beyond

There being no suitable National Army training facilities in existence in June 1917, the government chose sixteen sites across the country upon which to erect cantonments, or training centers. One of them, Camp Upton, was located seventy-five miles east of Manhattan at a tiny hamlet called Yaphank. Getting there required a lengthy trip on the Long Island Railroad, the same line acquired by Conrad Poppenhusen in 1874. When the first draftees arrived from College Point, and other parts of New York City, they exited the cars, only to begin another march. This one took them to their final destination via roads that could be dusty or muddy, depending on the weather.

The camp was nowhere near being ready. Recruits had to spend much of their time clearing drill grounds of stumps and underbrush. [1] While a small number of two-story wooden shacks were scattered here and there, before long the great many piles of lumber strewn about, would be used in the construction of barracks. Each housed two hundred men. Work during that summer was slowed by extreme heat, rain and millions of mosquitos, but building took place at a rapid pace. In dry weather, walls of dust swept from end to end of the encampment. In wet weather, lakes inconveniently appeared. [2] During these, the earliest of days, a local recruit sent a letter to Draft Board 176 offering some pointers for the men, soon to be joining him at Camp Upton.

"For those who follow, it may be of interest that it will probably be at least a week before shoes and uniforms are given out. Consequently, it would be best to wear the most comfortable shoes one has. Also, a flannel shirt is better than a white shirt.

We have no lockers, so I suggest that the men's things be carried in a cardboard box or a tin breadbox. They can be used after camp is reached. A big nailbrush to scrub clothes with when washing them is handy, as is a clothes brush, for it is very dusty here. A small brush is another necessary item. There are stores here where such things can be bought by those who have not gotten them already." [3] It was good advice.

The first groups of College Point draftees had been treated to sumptuous farewell dinners. Sent off with dawn parades, the men were cheered on by thousands as they marched through the village to the railroad station, their peregrination culminating in special flag-raising celebrations. With feelings of pride tinged with sadness, perhaps a touch of anxiety, relatives and friends assembled there to see them off. [4] The Red Cross and Girl Pioneers gave comfort bags to each departing recruit. Fortified by magazines, cigars, and a few days worth of tobacco, [5] they boarded a train for the journey, last stop Camp Upton. Post-arrival, each was issued a mess kit, and fed the first of many army meals to come. They were then given a cot on which to sleep, and a tent in which to live. Welcome to the National Army.

The new soldiers were afforded an opportunity to choose a preferred branch of service, with attention paid to their individual background, skills and experience. For purposes of balance, transfers were made to insure that each company had an equal number of policemen, firemen, superintendents and cooks, stenographers, typists, mechanics and so on. Given a second physical, they were assigned to a regiment, then introduced to drilling, construction work, loading and unloading supplies, policing the camp, and KP; the inevitable kitchen police duty. [6]

As was typical, but by no means the rule, new recruits underwent five months of training in a variety of areas. They learned about gas, and how to avoid it; how to use a bayonet, and how to fire and maintain machine guns. The men were educated in the intricacies of sniping, and how best to employ the trench mortar; all a part of war, and in play on the battlefield. Training in these skills was provided by French and English Officers, all who had seen action in France on the Western Front. Herewith, they were gradually formed into fighting units of Uncle Sam's Army.

However much time was needed, or available, when their time came to move on, some soldiers were sent for additional training at Camp Meade in Maryland, Camp Wadsworth in South Carolina, or to sundry other locations. Others went directly to France. What was that like?

In the middle of any given day or night, units that had completed their stateside training, wherever it occurred, left their barracks. They boarded a train, and upon reaching their destination, walked up a gangplank onto a waiting steamship.

Before America's entry into the war, the North German Lloyd Steamship Company and the Hamburg-America Line, had built many of the vessels on which the Europe-bound soldiers sailed. Up to that time, the vessels had made regularly scheduled trips between Germany and New York. When war was formally declared, the United States Government seized any of German-flagged ships berthed at New York-area piers, and others. Transformed into troopships, the *Kaiser Wilhelm II* sailed under American colors, renamed the *Agamemnon*. So, too, did the *Necar*, now the *Antigone*, the *Rhein*, the *Susquehanna*, and the *Vaterland*, the *Leviathan*. There were others of course; the routine was always the same.

Alighting from the gangplank, the soldiers were immediately warned that due to the possibility of attack by submarines, they were not to throw anything overboard; not cigarette butts, not papers, and not food scraps. Matches, easily spotted when struck at night, were confiscated. Sleeping on cots was difficult. The men lived deep below deck, life preservers substituting for pillows. Quarters were dark, and poorly ventilated, plus occasional stormy weather only worsened what was already a bad situation. Lifebelts had to be worn at all times, bunks policed each and every day, and everyone had to be topside at 8:30 every morning, rain or shine.

A brief stop at Halifax, Nova Scotia was a prelude to joining a convoy of ships, one of them a mandatory American cruiser. Life on board was a succession of long days and nights, interrupted by drills, exercise and inspections. There was also bulkhead, guard and submarine watch, as the convoy made its nine to fourteen day journey, leisurely zigzagging across the ocean until reaching England, its final destination. [7]

This was every doughboy's trans-Atlantic experience, when submarines posed great threats to any ships at sea, and there was always a possibility that one might launch a torpedo before the English coastline came into view.

9

From England to France

Upon arrival in England, some units underwent up to two additional months of training, usually in a quiet sector. For others, departure to France took place in a matter of days, the surprised soldiers finding themselves on another train. This one was English, headed east to Dover. Another water-borne voyage would take them on a brief trip across the English Channel to France, perhaps to the port of Saint Nazaire. Calais was another possibility. Here each man was issued a steel helmet that became his constant companion, and a British rifle in exchange for his American rifle. He also was given a British-made gas mask. [1] Such was the case, because when the U.S. declared war, the Army not only lacked them; it also had no concrete plans to manufacture them. [2] That situation changed rapidly. By December, College Point's Kleinert Rubber Company had been contracted to do just that. [3]

Poison gas was probably the most feared of all weapons in World War One. It was indiscriminate, and could be used on the trenches even when no attack was going on. For all arriving American soldiers, this was very likely their very first experience with it. The majority of doughboys found themselves in a chemical combat environment, with only a minimal amount of defensive gas training. They had no idea what the training meant. [4]

A brief lecture would be followed by gas mask drill, one hour a day, five days a week, under close supervision by British instructors. [5] Why the repetition? Having dealt with gas and other forms of chemical warfare since the beginning of the war, the Brits had the knowledge. They also had tactical and defensive experience, critical to soldiers in the field. They knew a poison gas attack meant masks had to be put on as quickly as possible. If unsuccessful, the soldier could be in agony for days and weeks before he finally succumbed to his injuries. [6]

The German chemical arsenal included mustard gas, so-called because of its peculiar odor. One doughboy likened it to a rich candy, filled with perfumed soap. But its smell belied its effect, and it was not really a gas. In actuality, it was a volatile liquid that several hours after contact with the skin, would cause severe burns, blisters, nausea and vomiting. Sometimes these effects did not become apparent for up to twelve hours. Then it began to rot the body from within and without, the pain almost beyond endurance. Death, in severe cases, could take up to four or five weeks. Phosgene caused a slow death by asphyxiation. It had the stench of a barrel of rotten fish. Chlorine gas smelled like a mixture of pineapples and pepper, but it had the same result with the dying soldier remaining conscious to within five minutes of the end.[7] Both caused fluid to enter the lungs thereby preventing oxygen from reaching the blood. This resulted in blindness, severe coughing, purpled lips, loss of speech and massive agony.[8] More than a few College Point soldiers wrote home to say they'd been gassed. Most lived to talk about it; one did not.

Because of the role they played, some units were taught the intricacies of the Vickers machine gun, pretty much the British Army's standard rapid-fire weapon. It weighed slightly less than forty-four pounds and was mounted on a fifty-pound tripod. The weapon was also capable of firing 450 rounds per minute. While these guns were reliable and durable, they were considered unwieldy as a battlefield infantry weapon. The Vickers could not be readily transported without great effort, plus it usually required a team of six men to operate the gun. Still, it was an effective killing machine all the new boys had to learn, not only how to fire, but also how to incorporate battlefield tactics so as to use it to its greatest possible effect.[9] Overall, the machine gun killed more soldiers than any other weapon used in the war.

To the extent possible, soldiers on both sides of the Atlantic got whatever preparation and training was needed to do a particular job. College Point men learned how to load, aim and fire heavy artillery. Some were taught to operate a tank, work a telegraph or shoe a horse others to butcher meat, cook meals or bake bread. They drove ambulances, served as orderlies, delivered and sent soldiers' mail, and censored their letters. A number worked in aero squadrons; some were billeted to flying school. They worked as quartermasters, at chemical warfare and intelligence; felled trees and repaired roads, while others entertained, played the bugle or registered graves. This was the army at war; there were numberless roles to fill, and jobs to do.

The units were frequently on the move in France. When possible, they rode in uncomfortable trucks, or when necessary, they marched. They frequently traveled by rail in the oftentimes-smelly French boxcars marked Hommes 40, Chevaux 8. The cars were not large. They measured twenty and a half feet long, by eight and a half feet wide, half the size of American boxcars. The French version was officially able to hold forty men or eight horses, "officially" being the operative word. [10]

Along the way, and after they arrived at wherever they were going, the men did enjoy some happy times. They discovered the joys of dining in small French cafés where they feasted on *les omelettes avec fromage ou jambon et pommes frites*, an omelet with cheese or ham and fried potatoes washed down with a glass of *vin rouge* or *vin blanc* complaining all the while that they were being charged more than were the French soldiers. *Poilus* they were called, literally "the hairy ones." [11]

They also suffered what would become typical of American solders' experience, life that morphed into months of mind-numbing boredom interrupted only by the chaos and sheer terror of going over the top into no man's land where men with guns large and small shot at them, and there was always the possibility of being bayoneted. They saw tanks up close, enemy aeroplanes overhead, and heard the crash of heavy artillery. They were bombed, gassed and made targets for the occasional "potato masher" or German hand grenade. [12] Sometimes they even found themselves in hand-to-hand combat, whatever it took to follow Major General John O'Ryan's orders given to the machine gun units of the 27th Division.

1. Your position will be held, and the section will remain here until relieved.

2. The enemy cannot be allowed to interfere with this program.

3. If the gun team cannot remain here alive, it will remain here dead, but in any case it will remain here.

4. Should any man, through shell shock or any other cause, attempt to surrender, he will remain here dead.

5. Should the gun be put out of action, the team will use rifles, revolvers, grenades and other novelties.

6. Finally, the position, as stated, will be held. [13]

10

To Their
Everlasting Credit

G eneral John "Black Jack" Pershing arrived in Europe on June 13, 1917 charged with preparing an American force able to take the offensive, in every way possible, against the central powers, Germany, Austria-Hungary et al. Two weeks later, to their everlasting credit, the first American contingent of soldiers arrived.

To their great relief, the doughboys were coming to the rescue of the allied powers, England and France, but the question remained, had they arrived in time? Estimates leaned toward four million men being needed. In less than nineteen months, under the draft system, the U.S. enrolled 24,000,000 men, but only 2,800,000 were mobilized. Of these, 2,000,000 were sent to France by July 4, 1918. By far, New York State had sent the most soldiers. According to Military Service Records, an infinitesimal percentage of them, slightly over 150, hailed from College Point.

In the first three months of 1918, the deaths of five local men would be reported. Their years of birth ranged from 1889 to 1899, and all had German blood flowing through their veins. There were two Catholics, two Lutherans and one Episcopalian. The five had nothing in common in terms of occupation, nor did they live in close proximity to one another. Though all resided in and had entered the service from College Point, there was little likelihood they had ever met.

The first died in battle, but had few if any significant connections to the community. The second would have the ties, but not the physical and perhaps emotional strength, to endure army life. Though techincally termed as having been killed in action, the third man's death would be more accurately described as the result of a friendly fire incident that occurred due to his questionable and highly irregular actions in a time of war. Death number four took place when a well-liked, and highly regarded sailor who had enlisted in 1913, lost his life in a tragic shipboard accident. His death was followed five days later, when a 19 year-old, not yet three weeks in the army, fell victim to a scourge that would kill millions around the world six months in the future.

The village mourned the loss of its first heroes with appropriate, and much deserved, recognition. Their stories follow.

11

George Andrew Rauh

April 15, 1892 - January 30, 1918

The year 1918 was not yet one month old, when on January 30th, George Andrew Rauh, first born son of a German immigrant named John Rauh, and his wife Wilhelmina, was listed as having been killed in a trench raid. [1] In his report, Anton Trostnski, a Sergeant in Rauh's company wrote, "I saw Private Rauh get hit by a shell from a trench mortar and die from his wounds. This occurred at Beaumont on January 30, 1918." Both legs were broken when the mortar shell burst, and his jaw was blown away.[2] Wrapped in a blanket, his uniformed body was buried in the American Cemetery at Mandres-Meurthe, then later moved to St. Mihiel American Cemetery in Thiacourt, France. [3]

George had attended school in Williamsburgh, and was employed at an unnamed Brooklyn glass factory in 1910. Sometime after 1915, he moved to College Point with his father, both probably seeking better jobs. His mother, two brothers and five sisters did not accompany them. On St. Patrick's Day, 1917, George enlisted in the Regular Army and assigned to the 7th Infantry. [4] Prior to that time, he had worked in a Brooklyn coal factory and lived with his sister, Catherine Lang, and her husband Fred. [5] In a letter to her he wrote, "I am going to give a good account of myself. My family will always be proud of my record." [6]

Following arrival in France in late June, he was transferred to the 18th Infantry as part of the First Division. It had acquired that nickname because it had been, "the first division in France; first to fire a shot at the Germans; first to attack; first to conduct a raid, and to be raided; first to capture prisoners; first to suffer casualties, and last to leave the war zone." [7]

In a letter to his father, he asked him to save the money coming to him from the government, so that he would have something with which to start a business when the war was over." In another to his sister, George told her, "I am proud to be a soldier. We are ready for the other fellows, whenever they come." [8]

A telegram addressed to John Rauh, arrived early in February. It told of his son's death, and was followed shortly thereafter by a form letter from the government saying, "Bodies of deceased soldiers will not be shipped from France to the United States during the continuance of the war. However, if in the future it is found to be practicable to ship the remains home in accordance with your request, it will be done. Steps will be taken to mark the grave of each soldier, to register the number and location of the grave, and to establish their identity beyond a doubt, should it become desirable subsequently, to disinter the remains for removal to the United States." [9] After discussing the matter with his family, John Rauh replied, "As the body cannot be sent at the present time, please leave his body at France." [10]

When the government offered to have his remains returned to the United States, the Rauh family made its wishes known. In early April 1922, following a Solemn Requiem Mass at his Catholic parish in Brooklyn, George Andrew Rauh was buried with full military honors in Cypress Hills National Cemetery. [11] Though born and raised beyond its borders, George

Andrew Rauh, he who had had made good on the promise made to his sister, was truly the first man with ties to College Point, to die in World War One.

12

Rudolph Brugger

October 14, 1889 - February 23, 1918

R udolph Brugger's mother Christine, was German; his father William, Swiss. Before his death in 1910, William Brugger had been a principal in the silk-dyeing firm of Brugger and Wehril. Growing up in College Point together with four sisters, Rudolph attended local schools and was employed by the New York City Parks Department on draft registration day, 1917. [1]

When examined by the physicians of Local Board 176, one of them, Dr. Alfred Ambler, refused to pass him. He was also the family physician, and knew Rudolph had been suffering from blood clots in his legs for some time. He believed the situation to be so bad that it would be impossible for him to take part in any drills at camp. The other physicians, however, certified him, as did army surgeons. [2] Inducted on September 29, he was sent to Camp Upton, and assigned to Company H, 306th Infantry. He was subsequently transferred to the 319th Field Artillery, Battery B, a machine gun company. His training continued at Camp Gordon in Georgia.[3]

With the macabre sense of humor typical of soldiers at the time, machine gun companies were called "suicide clubs". Such was the case because machine gunners stood in the forefront of fighting, sure to be special targets for enemy snipers and sharpshooters.[4] It is not known if Rudolph's company had been so designated.

Supported by letters written by Ambler, Brugger had made application for release from the Army, but while his application was under consideration, no determination had as yet been made.[5] A letter received at home showed him to be very despondent, so much so that he actually forgot to sign it.[6] In light of what transpired, Ambler's efforts went for naught. On February 25, 1918, Private Rudolph Brugger committed suicide by cutting his throat with a razor. It was a wound sufficient to have caused instantaneous death.[7]

Several men of his company had discovered his body in the barracks, but in the absence of his commanding officer, no details surrounding his death were released.[8] Hours after the grim discovery, his mother received a telegram announcing his death attributed to a complication of diseases.[9] Sadly, she soon learned the facts surrounding the manner in which he died.

His remains were shipped from Camp Gordon to College Point on February 27th, followed by an afternoon service held two days later at his mother's home. It was attended by many relatives and friends. A squad of soldiers from nearby Fort Totten accompanied the flag-draped coffin to Flushing Cemetery, where full military honors were accorded.[10] Christine Brugger passed away in 1931, and was buried in the same cemetery, most likely with her son.

13

Oscar Ammann

August 17, 1899 - March 7, 1918

O scar Ammann would be the youngest College Point soldier to die over the course of World War One. All deaths in a time of war are sad, but his touched the village deeply. He was only eighteen, nearly six feet tall, a strapping young man with black hair. Just three weeks before his death he had written home to say, "I am in excellent health, enjoying army life, and also hoping to return home some day with medals for valor in serving Uncle Sam." [1]

There had been no waiting around for the draft for Oscar Ammann. Ten days after President Wilson formally announced America's declaration of war, he left his job at the Kleinert Rubber Company to enlist in Company H, 12th New York National Guard Infantry. Four days earlier, another College Point youth, Lawrence Trimble, had done the same. He would be seriously wounded in September 1918. [2] Not only would he survive the injury, patriot that he was, Trimble would re-enlist to fight the Nazis twenty-six years later. Brothers Frank and William Baumert had enlisted three days before Ammann and Trimble, but not in the same unit. [3] Both would be reported as having been killed in action in early September, but much to their family's relief, those reports were in error. [4]

After arriving at Fort Wadsworth in Spartanburg, South Carolina, the Public School 27, class of 1915 graduate was transferred into Company F of the 165th Infantry, formerly the 69th New York. This was the famed Civil War Irish Brigade, now part of the Rainbow Division. Composed of hand picked National Guard units from 26 states and the District of Columbia, Colonel Douglas MacArthur, who had been instrumental in the forming of the Division remarked, "The 42nd Division stretches like a Rainbow from one end of America to the other." [5]

Between enlisting in April, and departing for France in late October, the Ammann family had what was very likely a difficult conversation. Never thinking it would come to pass, but aware he could lose his life in battle, a decision was required. Oscar, his parents Emil and Paula, and perhaps his younger siblings Harold and Loretta, decided his body would stay buried in France.

On the one-year anniversary of America's entry into the war, Paula, a native of Germany, received a letter from Michael A. Kelly, Captain of the 165th. "It is my very unpleasant duty to inform you of the death of your son, Private Oscar Ammon, [sic] which occurred as the result of a rifle wound, received in the line of duty. [6] Although he was grief-stricken, Oscar's father John expressed pride that his son should have been killed in defense of his country. [7] Other than Captain Kelly's letter, there is no way to know how much the Ammann's, or anyone in the community, knew of the circumstances surrounding the young soldier's death.

The initial report filed in the National Archives at College Park, Maryland reads, "Private Oscar Ammann was shot through the left breast by Private Bernard Corcoran, who was on sentry duty in a trench near the village of Souchet. The shooting took place at about 9:00 P.M. There was some excitement since the garrison had fired several shots prior to the accident. Private Ammann died a few minutes after the shooting while being carried to a first aid station." [8] Twenty-six year-old Corcoran was an Irish immigrant who had lived, and worked in Astoria prior to the war.

According to reports, Ammann was wearing a German spiked helmet called a pickelhaube, while bringing ammunition to a trench in front of the battlefield. In the darkness, and thinking the trench had been infiltrated by an enemy combatant, Corcoran, who had pulled sentry duty that night, fired the fatal shot. Young Ammann, died instantly from a bullet wound to the chest. [9] Following this calamitous misfortune, the young soldier, according to Chaplain Francis P. Duffy, was buried in Grave #1 at the American Cemetery at Croixmare, in the village of Romagne. [10]

In his memoirs written after the war, Father Duffy wrote, "The bodies of Eddie Kelly and Oscar Ammon [sic] of Company F were buried in Croixmare in a plot near a roadside Calvary which, from the trees surrounding it, was called the "Croix de L'Arbre Vert" or "Cross of the Green Tree." Over the ruined dugout we erected a marble tablet with the inscription, "Here on the field of honor rest." [11] It was followed by their names.

Duffy visited the cemetery on Memorial Day, noticing that "French villagers had erected a simple fence, and planted a hedge with flowers and vines. The Chaplain collected children from the village, and together, they decorated each cross with flowers" [12]

It was not long after reading of Oscar's death in France that those who claimed him as one of their own, acknowledged his loss. In early May, on the 50th Anniversary of the founding of the Poppenhusen Institute, a commemorative flag was presented. On it had been sewn 150 stars, each representing former students serving in the armed forces. A big blue star in the center shone a silent tribute to one who had died, Oscar Ammann. He was identified as being the first Institute's students to give his life for his country. [13] Similarly, a month later St. Fidelis held a three day celebration of Flag Day, part of which was another memorial service. In the ceremony, four Boy Scouts carried a golden star into the church in commemoration of Oscar Ammann. He had earlier been identified as having been a parishioner. [14] When the service flag was raised at Public School 27, the name at the top of the list of those who had lost their lives, was that of Oscar Ammann. [15]

When the war ended, his remains were removed from their original burial site, and reinterred in the Meuse-Argonne American Cemetery. Emil Ammann sailed to Europe in the summer of 1921 to visit the home of his parents in Switzerland. He then traveled on to France to pray at Oscar's grave. [16] Paula did not make the trip. In 1929, however, the United States Government arranged for mothers and widows of fallen soldiers to visit the graves of their beloved husbands and sons. Called the Gold Star Mothers' Pilgrimage, Paula Ammann took advantage of the offer. [17]

Ironically and sadly, Corcoran, the soldier whose rifle shot brought about Oscar's death, was himself wounded during the war. About him Chaplain Duffy wrote, "He got a bullet across both his eyeballs, which will render him blind for life." [18]

Francis P. Duffy was a Catholic priest in the Archdiocese of New York who had previously done chaplain service in the Spanish-American War. At the onset of World War One, he was given permission to reenlist in his old outfit, the famous Fighting 69th Infantry. Of him it was said, he knew by sight and by name every one of the men in the unit, and to have loved and delighted in them all. He returned to parish life after the war, and served a church in Times Square unitl his death in 1932. Five years thereon, Mayor Fiorello LaGuardia, who would spend that summer doing the city's work at the Chisholm Mansion in College Point, presided over the dedication of a statue in the same Times Square to honor the memory of the most highly decorated cleric in the history of the U.S. Army.[19] Three years later actor Pat O'Brien would portray the chaplain in the movie titled *The Fighting 69th*. His co-star was actor James Cagney.

Paula Ammann passed away in College Point on December 8, 1947. Emil continued to work at the Kleinert factory, where he had once toiled alongside his son. He died in March 1954. Both are buried in Flushing Cemetery. Oscar's memory endures; Ammann American Legion Post No. 853 is still very much a part of College Point life.

14

William Emil Buerger

January 10, 1897 - March 9, 1918

William Emil Buerger was on the cusp of turning seventeen on November 23, 1913. It was also on this day that his career in the U. S. Navy began. [1] He had only two and a half years earlier graduated from elementary school, [2] but it was not a time of celebration for him or his family. Emil Buerger, his father, had just died. He was 46. [3] Emily Buerger was left with three young children. Emily, called Minnie, was fifteen; William, fourteen, and Fred, the youngest, nine. With the breadwinner gone and the family in straits, his decision to enlist was not altogther unwelcome.

His first tour of duty was for a period of a little over three years. At 6'1", with brown eyes and hair, he was a good and capable sailor. By the time he was honorably discharged in January 1917, he had served aboard six ships, the *USS Constellation,* used for training in Newport, Rhode Island,

and battleships *Georgia, New Jersey, New Hampshire, Illinois* and *Rhode Island*. [4] He was top rated, scoring 4.0 for sobriety, 3.2 in terms of obedience and 3.6 as a leader of men. In good navy tradition, he had also gotten himself tattooed. On his left arm he sported a dragon and a dagger, "Babe R" and the phrase "Death before Dishonor." On his right was etched a star, a cross and the phase, "In Memory of Father" / "Never Part", and the initials, "TJR", USN and WEB". In Memory of Father, USN and WEB are easy to decipher. The others are open to conjecture, but otherwise unexplainable. [5]

The navy liked William E. Buerger, and he enjoyed the life of a sailor, so on January 30, 1917, he reenlisted. [6] The day also marked the one-week anniversary of his mother's marriage to Gustave Manther, a German-born machinist. [7] Disregarding the new circumstances of his mother's life, William arranged for a voluntary monthly allotment of $15.00 out of his pay, to go to her. At the same time, in the unlikely event he should die while in the Navy, he named her and his now married sister Minnie V. Boymann, as beneficiaries on $5,000 insurance policies. [8]

In April, William was ordered to the six-year-old *USS Burrows*, a destroyer called a "four piper" because it had four smokestacks. Following commissioning in 1911, the ship had served along America's Atlantic coast from New England to Florida, in and around the Caribbean. She steamed across the Atlantic to France in June, but was soon sent to Queenstown on the south coast of Ireland. It became the ship's base for nearly a year. [9]

William served his country well and was promoted to the rank of coxswain. His ratings in all aspects of navy life were consistently 3.0 or better, except for an occasional 2.5, which he got in signaling. As for conduct and sobriety, he was always rated 4.0 and recommended both for the good conduct medal, and for reenlistment. [10]

The telegram his mother received was simple and straightforward. "The Bureau regrets to inform you that your son William Emil Buerger seaman USN, died today at a Naval Hospital Haulbowline, a facility of the Irish Navy, from a fractured skull as the result of a fall from a smokestack of the *USS Burrows*." Officially, the death occurred at 8:30 p.m. on March 9th with the explanation, "While working on the deck of this vessel on March 8, 1918, a staging fell from one of the funnels striking him, and throwing him to the deck. He was transferred to *USS Dixie* in a semi-conscious condition, and was at once transferred to the Royal Naval Hospital, Base Six in Queenstown, Ireland. A Board of Inquest found that he had died as a result of fracture of the skull, origin in the line of duty, and not the result of his own misconduct." He had not fallen from the stack, rather the staging around it had fallen upon him. His effects were sold at auction, and the total amount sent to the ship supply officer. Everything else, "trinkets, keepsakes and papers", were forwarded to his mother by registered mail. [11]

Twelve days before his fatal accident, the College Point Chapter of the American Red Cross received a letter he had sent dated February 27th. In it Buerger wrote, "Dear Friends, Received another of your packages from the women folks of College Point containing socks and helmets and must say I appreciate the little token very much and will give my thanks to all concerned. I must say every little bit helps to make life more pleasant over here. It is going on nine months since we left New York, and we have no hope of seeing College Point for nine more, at least from what we hear from newspapers. But as all our friends are devoting their time to the welfare of the boys over here, time does not seem to drag. So thanking again for your kindness and with my best wishes and regards, I'll close and remain a pleased sailor. [12]

William Buerger's body was shipped to New York aboard the *USS Bridge*, and buried in Flushing Cemetery on Friday April 12th. It is unlikely his brother Fred stood among the mourners, for he was at sea transporting soldiers to and from the battlefields of France. He had joined the navy in early June, completed his basic training in September. Following a month aboard the battleship *Oklahoma*, destined to be torpedoed and sunk at Pearl Harbor, he was ordered to the *Powhatan*, a U.S. Army transport ship. [13]

A few weeks after the funeral, William's mother and sister were informed that as of an Act of Congress dated October 8, 1917, each was entitled to receive monthly insurance payments of $28.70 beginning March 10, 1918 through the same day in 1938. [14] This amount, roughly $400.00

in today's dollars, had to have been of great benefit in the Depression years that followed.

By all measurements, William Emil Buerger had lived the military life longer than would any of his peers. Long after the war had ended, in recognition of his service, and brother Fred's as well, each was awarded the Victory Medal and Lapel Button. Both were secured by Gustave Manther, who himself had enlisted in the Navy in December 1900. Acknowledging receipt of the decorations from the Navy Department, he wrote, "It is my utmost desire to express my sincere thanks and God's blessing to our beloved country and its glorious Flag under which we live." [15] Divorced from Emily at this time, it can only be surmised he had secured the medals and lapel pins on her behalf. As late as 1928, Emily had been in contact with the Navy to advise that she was now living with her daughter Minnie's family in Sullivan County, New York. [16] Since she does not appear in their household in the 1930 census, it is likely she died in the interim.

15

Charles O. Mahler

January 3, 1893 - March 14, 1918

Following almost immediately the reports that Ammann and Buerger had died, a short newspaper insert appeared saying another of College Point's sons, 25 year-old Charles O. Mahler, had passed away in the hospital at Camp Upton. [1] Assigned to Company C, 302nd Engineers, Mahler had been in the service for all of seventeen days. It was so short in duration that an Army serial number was either never assigned, or not recorded. [2]

On the day he registered for the draft, he was working as a shoemaker at College Point's Top Notch Shoe Company, [3] but before induction in late February, Charles had taken another job at the American Hard Rubber Company. Not long after arriving at Yaphank, he fell ill with lobar pneumonia. His death took place on March 14th. [4] Unknown at the time, Charles Mahler's death may well have been a harbinger of the epidemic that would encompass the world, killing millions of mostly young people later that fall, into early 1919. Influenza was the culprit; the so-called Spanish Flu.

College Point undertaker C. Johann and Sons, in business since post-Civil War days, brought his remains to the family home. Five days following his death, a military escort led the cortege to Flushing Cemetery where in a Lutheran service conducted by Rev. Arthur Halfmann, Charles' body was laid to rest. [5] Included among the mourners were his mother Rose, his father Henry and seven siblings. One of them was an older brother named Henry. Seven months after his brother's funeral, he would be drafted, spend a year in France and return home safely. [6]

The Mahler family immigrated to America from Germany in 1836. They settled in Manhattan, then moved to College Point before the start of the Civil War. Charles' grandparents had worked in Poppenhusen's rubber factory; his parents, for the founder's railroad. [7] When it became time for schooling, Charles attended and graduated from P. S. 27. As had many of his contemporaries, he took advantage of free classes at the Poppenhusen Institute, taking courses in woodworking and shop. Charles enjoyed sports, bowling in particular, representing St. John's Lutheran Church at various competitions.

On the day of his burial, the church dedicated a 36-star service flag honoring the men from the congregation serving in the armed forces. One of them was for Charles O. Mahler, [8] who had never fired his weapon in anger, but who nevertheless had died in service to his country. His unit, the 302nd Engineers, included fellow College Point men, Frank Braun, Louis Doerr, George Field, Paul Hubert, and John Messbauer. They left for France, two weeks to the day of his passing. [9] Come September, one of these five men would die in the Argonne Forest. Charles Mahler's parents remained in College Point. His father Henry, died in 1938; his mother Rose, in 1950.

16

I Long to Go Home

The American Army presence in Europe increased by 638,000 between the start of April, and the end of June 1918. joining the 14,000 who had come in May and June a year earlier. A microcosmic number of them, eighty-five, came from College Point.

At this time, the village, like others located across the borough of Queens was experiencing boom times. With its many factories, jobs were plentiful and good workers, in demand. At the same time, they were hard to come by. Whereas in peacetime, many of these businesses would have been manufacturing everyday necessities, and some luxuries. But with the war on, they were heavily engaged in fulfilling government contracts requiring day and night shifts to keep up with the demand. "Were it not for the strict censorship over such matters, I could tell you a great deal of the activities here now," said John W. Rapp. "The utmost caution must be taken." [1]

Precaution had become a regular part of life in this growing industrial center of the borough, even to the point of some individuals taking bizarre measures. Shortly after Congress had declared war in April 1917, fifty-five year-old Barney McKenna established his own personal war zone "about his castle, from which "alien enemies" were barred." It seems McKenna, whose son Patrick would depart for France in October 1918, had a next-door neighbor who happened to be Austrian. McKenna decided that if Uncle Sam could prohibit Austrians and Germans from residing in certain localities, then he had ample authority to prohibit his neighbor from walking on the sidewalk in front of his house. So he proceeded to place boards across the walkway at each end of his property, and posted a sign that read, "War Zone – Keep Out." The Austrian neighbor decided to ignore the sign and invaded McKenna's "war zone" using neither a submarine, nor an airplane. He just walked into the zone, only to find McKenna, "sitting all over him." The set-upon neighbor took his assailant to court where the magistrate fined Barney McKenna $10.00, warning him to establish his own little war zone in places where no one except himself would be likely to invade. [2] The invasive Austrian moved out before 1920, when the census-taker came to call.

The unresolved issue of what to do with aliens who had entered military service, the army in particular, was solved in part, when, toward the end of May, 500 foreign-born men clad in olive drab uniform, swore allegiance to the United States of America at Camp Upton. Reports indicated all had done so willingly, though breakdowns by nationality were not provided. One Italian was heard to say, "Now I feel I can fight twice as hard for the flag" and naturalization, a process that normally took up to seven years, was accomplished in a very few hours. [3]

By this time, anti-German sentiment had fairly well settled in, especially when it came to the publication of German language newspapers, once a profitable business in College Point. The whole country was strongly opposed to their existence. Twelve German newspapers across the county had suspended publication. On Long Island, Oyster Bay citizens asked its newspaper vendors to cease selling them. Other towns and localities, Glen Cove and Hempstead among them, had done similarly. Many cities in neighboring New Jersey banned them altogether, and the publishing house of G. P. Putnam Sons announced it would publish no work tinged with German, for the next twenty-five years. Circulation of books published in German had fallen off in the New York City Public Library. [4]

While all this was going on, College Point soldier Albert Frey, whose father Edward had once published a German language paper called *Die Freie Presse*, had just arrived in France. There he would lay down his life.

With at least eighty-five of its men having departed for French battlefields in the second three months of the year, there had to have been many tearful farewells in College Point. Some took place with only a day's notice. Not everyone got a massive send-off parade, and generally speaking, individual soldiers bade goodbye to their families and friends in a hurried fashion. The next time they would be heard from would be via post cards written at the time of departure, and mailed on this side of the water by the government, upon notice of safe arrival in France.

In addition to the postcards, newspapers began reprinting selected letters from soldiers one among them a mid-June missive from College Pointer, Henry Dillmann, Jr., serving with the 18th Infantry in France. Written from his hospital bed to friends back home at the Adelphi Social Club in College Point, it read:

"Just a few lines letting you know I am getting well and feeling much better. I have been up in the trenches for the first time and was very lucky. I was gassed one night while in the trenches. It was that mustard gas that leaves burns wherever it gets you, and I've been burnt all over the body and my eyes also. I'm in the hospital now, but am improving daily.

We were in a dugout singing the latest songs when the Germans made the gas attack, and we had to leave our gas masks on for seven hours. It was a mean job. Nobody knows what it is to be up in the trenches, but they soon find out. It makes an altogether different fellow out of you, for it is man to man.

The hospital I am in is a very good one. One thing I will say is the Red Cross is certainly doing its bit for the boys over here. I wish you would make a note for the reporter of The Times letting the people know what I think of the Red Cross and that I send my best love and regards to the Red Cross workers of College Point. Many a long time I long to go home and attend some of the meetings. I hope the time will come soon that I will be able to be with you again, for I always think of the good times I had with the Adelphi Social Club. Convey my best regards to all members of the club. [5] To this point in time, the College Point Red Cross had raised almost $15,000. [6] The Adelphi Social Club was formed in 1889. [7]

Support for the war, and for everyone serving in America's armed forces, was strong across the country. The Red Cross, YMCA and YWCA in association with the Salvation Army, Jewish Welfare Board, American

Library Association and Knights of Columbus planned independent campaigns. Their objective was, not only to raise money, but also to assist the soldiers and civilian populations impacted by the war. By the close of December 1917, St. Ambrose Council Knights of Columbus in College Point had raised $360,000, [8] and when advanced degrees were awarded to one hundred candidates early in 1918, more than half were in uniform. [9]

While the family of Alfred Fagan was staunchly Catholic, there is no record that a Fagan son named Thomas had ever been a Knight of Columbus. He did, however, join the army in July 1917, not the American army, but the Canadian army. Thus began a military sojourn that would have its end in France, slightly less than a year later. He got to say goodbye to his family, as did Alfred Stengel, who in September, was among the first draftees from the village to embark for Camp Upton, and then go on to France. Their stories follow.

17

Thomas Henry Fagan

February 12, 1899 - June 6, 1918

Thomas Henry Fagan was fifteen when war broke out in Europe. Three years later, old enough to serve, but not to register for the draft, he took the train to Manhattan to enlist in the Army. But it was not to be. Rejected beause he was not an American citizen, Thomas right away boarded a train for Toronto. There, on June 19, 1917, he enlisted in the 48th Canadian Highlanders. [1.] He was, after all, a citizen of Great Britain. His parents, taken by surprise with his abrupt departure, considered an attempt at talking him out of his decision, but knew all too well, his mind was set.

The eighteen year-old enlistee was born in Manchester, England, on February 12, 1899, the third child of Alfred and Mary Fagan. His mother was born in County Cork, his father in Manchester. Both had immigrated to America in the early 1890's. They met in Manhattan and married in 1894. Following the birth of two sons, John and Leo, they departed for England and Alfred's hometown, the northern city of Manchester.

The Fagan's returned to New York in 1901, eventually settling in College Point. By 1910, they were living in a house Alfred had built, big enough to hold them and their children, nine in number. The family home overlooked a small body of water called Powell's Cove; an idyllic location.

Thomas belonged to the Young Men's Catholic Lyceum, [2] a sports association of St. Fidelis Church, where Father George Bittermann, a young parish priest, coached the boys. Unlike his brothers who preferred the local dance halls, Thomas had more a serious bent. He attended Mass regularly, and always received Communion. Graduating from P.S. 27, he was considered a model student, artistic by nature. [3] He even took courses in drawing and design at the Poppenhusen Institute. [4]

July, August and September found recruit Thomas in training at Camp Borden in Ontario. In October, he was granted leave to spend time in College Point, reuniting with family and friends before returning to his regiment. On his final day at home, while walking to the train station, Thomas spoke quitely with his younger sister Ellen, saying to her, "I've got a feeling I'm not coming back." She protested, "Nothing's going to happen." Before boarding his train, he took his father aside. Speaking once more in hushed tones, he relayed the same message, adding his concern for his mother, should his fears come to pass. As the train departed, father and daughter waved their goodbyes, then walked together down the platform headed for home. Neither spoke of their intimate conversation with son and brother until years later.

The Highlanders shiped out at the end of November. Upon reaching Europe's shores, his mother received a Christmas present of sorts, notice that Thomas had arrived safely in England. [5] Three months later, on March 30th, young Tommy was selected to train with the Machine Gun Corps.

In all, Thomas Fagan wrote twenty-four letters home, most of which began with either, "I'm feeling fine and dandy" or "I write to let you know I'm in the finest of health." All of the letters were kept, and cherished, by the Fagan family. He also kept a diary, his entries indicating he consumed a great deal of bread, jam, hardtack and tea, and the ever-present, "bully beef", canned corned beef that was also called monkey meat. Along with his mates, Tommy dug a lot of trenches in small French villages with names like Merville, Calonne and Vimy, trenches where troops were in constant danger of artillery, gas and snipers.

His final entry was written on May 30th at Aubin St. Vaast, near the Pas de Calais on the coast. Written just twenty-six days after the start of training, it reads simply, "Reveille at 6… breakfast at 6:30… drill from 8:30 till 12… afternoon route march in battle order… evening went to concert and cinema… One week later, the June 7th Report of the Commanding Officer, Canadian Machine Gun Corps had this entry, "Thomas Fagan, No. 2393387, Killed, Accidentally shot whilst undergoing instruction on Machine Gun."

Thomas was buried in the nearby British Cemetery at Huby St. Leu, an area made famous by the poem, *In Flanders Field* by John M. McCrae. A forty-two year-old Canadian physician, who himself had volunteered for service at the outbreak of the war, laid down his life in France. Its first line mentions the poppy, a flower that grows there in great numbers.

On June 19th, the first Western Union Telegram was delivered to Mary Fagan. "Deeply regret to inform you… Pte Thomas H. Fagan accidentally killed June 7, 1918." A second followed on July 24th, "Thomas Henry Fagan previously reported killed… now officially reported died of injuries accidentally received." The Fagan's had joined the growing numbers of College Point's grief stricken families, who had themselves received the same sad news.

"A Memorial Mass was held at St. Fidelis Church with Father Bittermann, the celebrant. Family and friends climbed the entrance steps. A bell tolled mournfully from the steeple. Inside, an Irish Catholic family gathered in a Gothic church filled with traces of its German roots. Stained glass windows bore the names of German donors, the church's first parishioners. Ironic, some thought. In the midst of all these German influences, an Allied casualty was being memorialized… a hometown boy, if not killed by the Germans, killed because of them."

When Mass was over they returned home... a home missing a child... a loss they would suffer for the rest of their days. With no other details forthcoming, for years Alfred and Mary Fagan anguished over confusing telegrams. They just wanted to know what had happened to their son, and the specifics of the accident that had taken his life. But they never did learn."

On December 30, 1934, Thomas' youngest sister Margaret married Joseph Eck. Their son Robert, born on in September, 1944, would, after years of ardent research, solve the mystery surrounding the death of his uncle, Thomas Fagan. It was a story he would write in great detail in an unpublished manuscript titled, *"Tommy, We'll Miss You Son."*

"This is how Thomas lost his life. On the morning of June 6, 1918, five squads of machine gun recruits were assembled for training on the Lewis Machine Gun. Secured cartridge belts of dummy ammunition were used for firing. Once ejected from the gun, the spent rounds were then reinserted in the belts. The day before, a number of live rounds had been found on the ground, their origin unknown. At the end of the day, when dummy rounds were retrieved for reuse, two live rounds were inadvertently inserted into the cartridge belts.

Between 11 A.M. and 12 Noon, Pte. D. Gash squeezed the trigger of his machine gun, heard a report and felt the shock. Another soldier having stepped back from his rank to take notes, had moved into the line of fire. A single round struck him and two others. Seriously wounded, the men fell backwards to the ground. Thomas, one of the three, died the following day. A Court of Inquiry declared he had lost his life in performance of his duty, fixing blame on no one. It had been an accident."

Alfred Fagan died on October 19, 1942. Mary outlived him, passing away eleven years later. Ill and often confused, still grieving as if the telegram had just arrived, sometimes she thought it was 1918. Robert J. Eck died in Roanoke, Virginia on April 16, 2006. Much of what appears in the preceding story is the result of his research. Of him it could easily be said, Robert, We'll Miss You, Son.

18

Alfred Stengel

August 12, 1893 - June 24, 1918

Located in a grove in Central Park in the back of the band shell at 69th Street is a war memorial. It honors the memory of the 590 men who fought and died in the First World War as members of the 307th Infantry Regiment of the 77th Division of the Allied Expeditionary Forces from New York. The area is marked, but it is very unobtrusive. [1]

Seven men from College Point served in the 307th. William L. Tuffin, married with two children, and on parole when drafted on September 19th, deserted two months later. [2] Five others, Theodore Stark, Edward Martin, John J. Barrett, Gustave Greiner and George A. Spaeth, [3] served their country well, and came home, though not altogether unscathed. The seventh man, Alfred Stengel, was not so blessed.

Three weeks before registration day, Alfred's younger brother Charles enlisted in the Regular Army. On 5 June 1917, Alfred did what his country required; he registered, filled out the form, and underwent the mandatory physical examination. He then reported to his job at a machine shop not far from his home. [4] Summer faded into fall. Alfred moved on to the College Point Boat Company, and was drafted on September 22nd [5] His friends gave him a hearty farewell with the music of drums and bugles stirring the air as they paraded up and down the streets. The procession finally came to an end at one of College Point's saloons, where a good time was had by all. [6] The next day, a Long Island Railroad train took him to Camp Upton, where he was assigned to the 307th Infantry. The following April, he was on his way to France with his unit. [7]

While his father John, a German immigrant, worked as a carpenter, his Swiss-born mother Martha, her two sons in the army, looked around for a way to do her part. In the fall, she joined a large number of ladies of College Point, some mothers, some wives, who had started a knitting club at the Poppenhusen Institute. [8] By the end of January, these seventy-five women would knit 541 garments. They were sent to 159 of the husbands and sons away in training; some already at war. [9] Martha Stengel had knitted, with "excellent workmanship", six sweaters, four mufflers, six pairs of wristlets, ten helmets and seventeen pairs of socks." Had records been kept of the many noble women who contributed to the war effort, the mother of Charles and Alfred Stengel would have at the least merited an honorable mention. [10]

As the 307th was making its way east across France in mid-June, they gave way to let soldiers from the 165th Infantry pass by. They were coming out of the front lines headed west to relative safety. [11] Presumably, Alfred was aware that Oscar Ammann, a member of the 165th, had been killed just three months earlier.

Not too long thereafter, the 307th was entrenched near the village of Neuviller. At three o'clock on the morning of June 24th, German artillery began a massive barrage. Shells containing gas, mustard and phosgene, poured down like hailstones. An hour later the attackers came in, the famous "Prussian Guards." [12] They were equipped with bombs, machine guns and flame-throwers spouting fire so intense that it bent the men's rifles. The men of the 307th, outnumbered ten to one, stuck bravely to their posts. They fought fiercely, desperately, and while they inflicted heavy losses on the attacking troops, some men were gassed, others captured; still others died. [13]

Theodore Stark was one of those gassed. He had done the one thing the trainer's had warned him against, removing the mask before knowing it was safe to do so. Stark went to the hospital and recovered to fight again. Edward Martin, who had married just weeks before being drafted, was among the first Americans to be captured by the Germans. He and Alfred had been friends for years. They were both drafted the same day, and were sent to the same camp for training. Most unusually, they were assigned to the same brigade, the same regiment and the same company. They had left for France on the same ship, and had gone into action side by side. [14] Martin was a bugler. He spent the next six months in a prisoner of war camp at Rastatt, near Darmstadt, Germany. [15]

Alfred Stengel died from wounds received. His uniformed body was buried in Grave #6, American Plot #1 in the French Military Cemetery in the village of Montigny. A Sergeant named Loftus assigned to the burial detail, had found that some of the victims had burned to death. [16] Without naming him specifically, Alfred was very likely among them. While his status as a graduate of P. S. 27 had already been acknowledged, in mid-July, St. John's Lutheran Church announced its service flag now contained 54 stars; one of them for Alfred Stengel. [17] June 24th had been a very bad day for men at war from College Point, but worse days were yet to come.

In an interesting sidebar, on the 24th of August, two months after Alfred's death, the 307th Infantry marched into a little valley east of a small village called Chery-Chartreuve. There, in a hole dug in the side of a cliff, was established the unit's regimental headquarters. Throughout the war, HQ's were given code names, and this one was designated "College Point."[18] It seems fairly reasonable to say that one of the men who served in the unit had a hand in suggesting it be called by the name of his home-town. It could also be considered a Great War version of "Kilroy was Here." During World War Two and the Korean War, Kilroy was the one person who led or participated in every combat, training or occupation operation. Always dependable, GI's during these two conflicts considered him the super GI. He was the one who always got there first, or who was always there when they left. [19] Fair to say, it was perhaps an apt description of a soldier from College Point in 1918.

Alfred's remains began their journey back home aboard the U.S. Army transport *Wheaton*. [20] A squad of soldiers escorted the body from Hoboken to College Point to C. Johann and Sons' funeral parlor. [21] On June 5th, four years to the day he had registered for the draft, his coffin was escorted to Flushing Cemetery by members of the Oscar Ammann American Legion Post. There he was laid to rest with full military honors. Mourners at the gravesite included his father and mother, brother Charles, and four younger sisters. [22] In his last letter written on June 15, 1918, nine days before his death, Alfred had indicated he expected to "go into the trenches soon." His father expressed the belief he had done just that, the day after he'd posted the letter. [23]

Not long after Alfred was buried, John and Martha Stengel moved from College Point to other parts of Queens. John passed away in late December 1938; Martha in September, 1953. Both are buried in Flushing Cemetery.

Edward Martin's time as a prisoner of war came to an end upon his release reported in early December, [24] almost a month after the armistice was signed. In the years to follow, he would serve as vice-commander of the Oscar Ammann Post playing Taps at military functions, and, of course, at veterans' funerals. Martin died in February 1938. [25]

19

July - September

Beginning with the Battle of Chateau-Thierry on July 18th, one of the first actions of Pershing's American Expeditionary Force, the months of July, August and September gave the Allies a series of almost unbroken victories across 450 miles of battlefront in France and in other parts of Europe. Austria-Hungary regarded the situation as being so desperate that on September 15th, she addressed a note to all belligerent and neutral powers inviting all those at war to send delegates for a "confidential, and unbinding discussion" on the basic principles for the conclusion of a peace, in a place in a neutral country and at a near date that would yet have to be agreed upon. [1] President Wilson rejected the proposal on September 17th, and the Allies continued to press on at great cost, moving eastward toward Germany.

In that same three-month period, even though victory might have appeared imminent, there was no such guaranty. Close to 860,000 more Americans crossed the Atlantic. A representative number of them were from College Point, where in July, police were investigating what appeared to be a bold attempt to harm employees of the L.W.F. Manufacturing Company. No conclusions were ever reported, [2] but it could be said that nerves were on edge.

During this time, families with German or Teutonic-sounding surnames began to change them to Anglicized versions. Schmidt morphed into Smith, for example, so as to alleviate any suspicion that might be cast. As the war years unfolded, anti-German hysteria manifested itself in bizarre, some would say foolish, ways. Sauerkraut was renamed Liberty Cabbage and frankfurters became "hot dogs" or "liberty sausage." City streets with German names, there were none in College Point, were doctored, as was Brooklyn's German Hospital. It became Wyckoff Heights Hospital. Even the Germania Life Insurance Company, one of the first to buy Liberty Bonds, had its name switched to the Guardian Life Insurance Company.

It was as if anything German had become anathema, even anti-American. The reasoning, however false, was simple. If something was pro-German, it had to be anti-American. Everything pro-German had to be eliminated; German newspapers, the German language, German clubs and German beer. Symphony orchestras refused to play the works of Beethoven, Bach and other German composers. While College Point could boast no orchestra on this scale, it had a long and well-earned reputation for excellent German church choirs, and choral groups. Their names reflected their origins, *maennerchor, damenchor* and *alpenroesli*. To the extent it is possible to know, the last reference to a *saengerfest*, meaning singing festival, being held in the village, appeared in mid-June 1915. [3]

The absurdity perhaps reached its zenith when a young boy's attempt to sell his daschund puppies through a Manhattan dealer, was rejected. His father received a letter telling him the dogs could not be sold at any price. Dealing in daschunds was looked upon as trading with the enemy, thus considered un-American. When the lad called for his puppies, the dealer offered him ten dollars for the young dogs. He took it. [4]

In hindsight, instances such as these could be classified as hysterical responses to threats, actual or perceived. In point of fact, such overreactions deeply affected the larger German-American community, though perhaps not as much in College Point, as in other parts of the country. Ample evidence exists to support the theory that the British and French governments did as much as possible to involve America in the war on their side. Promoting anti-German propaganda would not be, nor was it out of the question, in terms of their objective. [5]

At the end of July, 2,000 men departed for Camp Upton, seventy-two of them from Draft Board 176, thirty-three from College Point.[6] One month later, thirteen College Point recruits were sent to Camp

Gordon, Georgia. [7] They were soon to be joined by sixteen of their former friends, neighbors and co-workers. The majority of the sixty-two men had German heritage. One of them was William Schlichthorl. He had changed his name to William Slater. [8]

During the months of July, August and September, approximately sixty more College Pointers had landed in Europe. In terms of losses, August's newspapers noted the death of only one soldier from the village, John Harold Embree. September's story would be different. Eight would be killed in action over a five-day period in the Argonne Forest. Seven would die in October; four in battle, two due to influenza and one from appendicitis. Another would die from the same illness in November, yet one more from wounds received. The dying did not stop with the cessation of hostilities. Influenza contracted during the war would kill two more village men, one in 1919, and the other in 1920.

To be expected, the front pages of the nation's newspapers listed, by state, the names of the men killed, wounded or captured, and those dead by other causes, pneumonia or Influenza. By the fall of 1918, it was wreaking havoc around the globe irrespective of country. Soldiers were dying all along the western front in places called Noyon and Montdidier, and in major operations named for the French rivers near which they were taking place, the Somme, Oise-Aisne and the Marne. In mid-September, locations with names like St. Mihiel Salient appeared in large type headlines, replaced later that month by Meuse-Argonne, Montfaucon and the Hindenburg Line. Articles accompanied by maps described the battles that had taken place or were taking place, the charts pored over by parents, wives and siblings anxious for the welfare of their loved ones whose exact whereabouts were unknown. Strict letter censorship was in full force. In some cases, names of the dead and wounded were printed in newspapers before telegrams arrived.

The deaths of Lieutenant William A. Baumert, and his brother Frank, beloved sons of College Point cheese magnate William Baumert, had shocked the village. Frank's was reported in early September; William's much later. Terrible it was to lose one son; unimaginable to lose two in so short a span of time. Both were serving in the 105th Infantry. In the midst of planning memorial services, elation replaced grief when William's wife received a letter from him. It was dated subsequent to the date of death given in her telegram from the war department. In his letter, William told his wife that he had been gassed, that he was safe, and on his way to full recovery. Almost simultaneously, Frank Baumert's wife received a similar letter from her soldier husband. It was dated September 8th, clearly after his reported death on September 3rd. As was his brother, he wrote that he was in a hospital in France, also recovering from a gas attack. [9] "Bill and I are both all right. Don't worry." Lt. Frank Baumert was wounded in the face and leg, and in a letter to the boys' parents, William's Adjutant made special mention of his bravery under fire. The Baumert family's experience was the exception, sadly not the rule [10] as in the case of John Harold Embree.

20

John Harold Embree

May 2, 1898 - July 28, 1918

On May 8th, one month after America declared war on Germany, twenty year-old John Harold Embree, a 1916 graduate of Flushing High School and a student at Cornell University, enlisted in Company H, 7th Infantry, of the New York National Guard. Shortly thereafter, the unit became a part of Company K, 165th Infantry. This was the same Fighting Irish Brigade in which Oscar Ammann had served. Embree's training took place at Camp Mills on Long Island where John, called Harold by his family, was promoted to Private, 1st Class. He then shipped out for France on October 29th. The following December he made Corporal, and was then raised to the non-com rank of Sergeant in March 1918. [1]

It was in the little remembered Battle of the Ourcq River, not one that evokes strong images like those of D-Day or the Battle of the Bulge, that Sergeant Embree lost his life. Struck by a piece of shrapnel, as he swayed to one side a machine gun bullet struck him in the forehead, killing him instantly. [2] This took place seventy-five miles northeast of Paris, early in the two-month offensive, July 15 through September 16, 1918 that has come to be known as the Second Battle of the Marne. In its totality, the battle is important because it marked the turning of the tide in favor of the Allies in World War One. [3]

The objective was to cross the Ourcq, more a stream or creek than a river, capture the heights, the high ground to the north, and occupy what was called the Meurcy Farm. It was heavily fortified by German machine gun nests. The river crossing had its challenges, but the men of the 42nd Division to which the 165th Infantry was attached, were confident the objective could be attained.

Father Francis P. Duffy, whose statue stands in Times Square, described the action leading up to Embree's death. "The line was scarcely straightened out when the men were given the word to advance. The left of Company K moved out on the lower slopes along the little valley toward Meurcy Farm; the right of K and all of Company I at an angle straight up the bare, smooth slope towards the machine gun nests that were spitting fire from that direction. That kind of action suited Lieutenant Pat Dowling, second in command of Company K. He jumped to his feet and called to his platoon to follow when a machine gun bullet gave him a mortal wound. Sergeant Embree fell by his side." [4]

Before enlisting, Harold Embree was known among his friends to have been a very good boxer. Because of his skills, he had acquired the nickname Jeff. [5] At the time, a retired world heavyweight boxing champion named James Jeffries, was a popular figure. It is very likely the nickname was homage to the man who had fought and beaten, the big name fighters of the era, among them "Gentleman" Jim Corbett. At the time of his retirement from the ring, Jefferies had never been beaten. [6]

The nickname followed him to France thus explaining why the official Burial Record reads, "the body of "Jeff" Embree was initially buried in Grave # 97 near the mill at Meurcy Farm." Harold's remains were subsequently disinterred then reburied in a second site, the Oise-Aisne American Cemetery at Seringes-et-Nesles. Grave #105 was marked by a nameplate and cross to which was attached a quarter-size metal identification tag bearing his name, unit and rank. [7]

On the morning of August 9th, the telegram bearing the news arrived in College Point. Addressed to his father John G. Embree, it read, "Deeply regret to inform you that Sergeant John H. Embree Infantry is officially reported as killed in action July twenty-ninth. [8]

Early in January 1919, the Embree family received a letter from Harold's Company K Captain, John P. Hurley. His words undoubtedly touched them deeply. "Sergeant Embree was killed on the morning of July 28th about 4:15 A.M. as this Company at the head of the Rainbow Division crossed the Ourcq River. He was killed beside his platoon commander Lt. Dowling who lost his life that day. I believe he was administering aid to Lt. Dowling. We attacked at 4:05 A.M. and just as we cleared the river your son was shot, I believe by a sniper. He died almost instantly. In my experience I have seen but very few men as brave as your son, and I have never seen one more loyal. He was to have left that night for a training school for officers and you will be glad to know that his right to a commission was established by the only criterion by which a soldier should be judged - the battlefield." [9] Hurley was a Cornell graduate, class of 1907, but it is not likely he was aware of that connection to Embree.

Shortly after the war, a Company K Sergeant named Patrick J. Ryan from New York City, stopped in College Point. He was on a mission to return Harold's watch to his parents. The thoughtfulness was deeply appreciated, and in turn, John and Marie Embree gave the timepiece to Ryan. [10] Harold had been very close to a girl from Flushing named Cynthia York. The two were reportedly engaged at the time of his death. They had known each other since high school days, both having graduated in 1916. While Harold was a student at Cornell, Cynthia was attending Vassar.[11] Following his death, she was given dinner plates from a set of family china.[12] A decade later, she married in California. [13]

So typical of the times, letters that dealt with the return of the remains to America were sent back and forth, Army to John Embree, John Embree to the Army. In one, he noted, "My son was killed in action on July 28, 1918. Sometime before he had his photograph taken at Baccarat. There [sic] were probably in the mail for him. We have not received any of his personal effects and only a few of the letters that had been mailed to him. We are very anxious to get the photographs especially. Can you give any assistance?" [14]

Other letters included discussions of whether or not Harold's body would stay buried in France, or returned to the U.S. In the end, a choice was made. On August 4, 1921. his casket arrived in College Point, and a funeral service was held. Four days later his remains were buried at Arlington National Cemetery. [15] It was a fair day with temperatures in the mid 80's. At two-thirty in the afternoon, his body was re-interred a third, and final time, in Grave # 3265. A lone bugler played Taps, and the folded American flag was presented to his mother, Marie Wright Embree, undoubtedly mourning the loss of two much-loved men in her life.

Five weeks earlier, John G. Embree, Principal of the Poppenhusen Institute for fourteen years, organizer of the first Boy Scouts of America Troop in College Point, Chairman of the local and Queens County Red Cross, Chairman of the Local Liberty Loan Committee and unstintingly generous with his time and talents, died at the age of forty-eight following surgery in New York Hospital on June 27th. It was the same day on which his second son James Newlin Embree graduated from Flushing High School, [16] and almost three years to the day of Harold's death. While the official cause was attributed to a heart attack, many believed its true cause was grief over Harold's death. [17] His funeral was held at the Poppenhusen Institute. Every one of the village's clergymen took part, presiding, preaching or eulogizing the educator, patriot and civic worker. His body lay in state throughout the day guarded by members of the Oscar Amman Post of the American Legion, and all of the village's Boy Scout Troops. A male chorus sang "America" as an unending line of mourners passed by the bier. Following the ceremony, his remains were taken to his hometown, Marshallton, Pennsylvania, for interment. [18]

In May 1931, Cornell University dedicated an impressive memorial to honor 264 men from the university who had served during the war. Numbered among the 206 who had given their lives, was John Harold Embree. [19] Had he survived the war, he would have been in the graduating class of 1920. Marie Embree died in New Jersey on August 8, 1942, and is buried with her husband in Marshallton, PA.

21

August Bigler

September 7, 1888 - August 18, 1918

When the country called in 1917, thirty year-old August Bigler dutifully responded. He then returned to his job at the Kleinert rubber factory. A short time later, he and eleven other local men were drafted. One of them was his brother Jacob, younger by two years. [1] On December 8th, all of the new recruits rode the train to Yaphank to begin training for war. August, or "Gus" as he was fondly called, was assigned first to Company D in the 306th Infantry, but just prior to shipping out for France, he was reassigned to Company B in the 302nd Ammunition Train. [2] It was to be a life-altering event.

At the start of the war, the government's plan was to use horse-drawn carts to carry ammunition to fighting areas, but in a very short time, trucks got factored into the mix. Horses or trucks, it would still be Gus Bigler's army job to load, unload, guard and transport, the ammunition so necessary to the front line troops fighting the war. As the need for increased manpower in France increased, four months after arriving at Camp Upton, Gus found himself on a troop ship headed for Europe.

Commencing in April, his training was on-going, such that by the 1st of August, the 302nd Ammunition Train was considered as ready for any duties in the field, as might be encountered. Active fighting at the front began on August 4th when his unit moved to the Vesle sector near the village of Fismes. Two weeks later on August 18th, French forces, with the support of the 77th and other American troops, began the very successful Oise-Aisne campaign. It was on this first day's action that Gus Bigler fell. He didn't live long enough to witness the withdrawal of the German forces. August Bigler was killed delivering ammunition to the front line trenches, struck by a shell while doing his job.

The September 21st edition of the *New York Times* carried the names of fourteen New Yorkers recently killed in action at Chateau Thierry. Gus Bigler's name was on the list. One week earlier, the telegram reporting his death had already been delivered to his mother and father, his one brother George still living at home, and his three sisters, Mary, Lillian and Dorothy. [3] They were the ninth College Point family to receive the never-wanted War Department telegram, but there was no explanation to explain its delayed delivery. Early in October, the family was heartened to receive a letter of condolence from the chaplain of his regiment, Rev. William N. Killian. He was a Catholic priest from the Archdiocese of Philadelphia, and one of the first to volunteer at the outset of the war.

"It is my sad duty to confirm the news of the death of your son August who was engaged in the performance of his duty at the time. By an unfortunate chance, which rarely occurs, the truck in which he was returning after the delivery of some ammunition, was struck by a shell. August was badly injured and lived only a short time. We buried him the following day in a beautiful little cemetery near the field hospital. August was known as one of our good soldiers, one who spoke fondly of his home and family. He was always prompt and cheerful in carrying out every command." [4] It was every chaplain's duty to compose these letters; none of them an easy task.

August's body was buried in Grave 102, Row C in a cemetery in the French village of Fere en Tardenois. Marked by a cross, it was located about a mile and a half east of what would become the Oise-Aisne American Cemetery, the final resting place for 6,012 men who died in this vicinity during this, the war to end all wars. On his uniform, one shirt collar had an ornament with the letters USNA, United States National Army. On the other was the letter T indicating his service on an Ammunition Train. [5]

Two years and ten months later, on an unusually cool and overcast July 14th, Gus Bigler's remains were sent home aboard the U.S. Army transport *Wheaton*. [5] Soldiers were listed by their name on a ship manifest to retain their dignity. Their caskets were placed in shipping cases, covered with the American flag, and carefully placed in the ship's hold for return from the theater of war to the U. S. Following a funeral service conducted at the Bigler home by First Reformed Church pastor Rev. Henry Herge, the body of Gus Bigler was laid to rest in Flushing Cemetery. [6] His brother Jacob, with whom Gus had ridden to Camp Upton, was among the mourners escorted by a detachment of members from the Oscar Ammann American Legion Post. Having begun his own army service in the same 306th Infantry, Jacob had also been transferred before shipping out, spending most of his time in the 148th and 121st Machine Gun Battalions. The December 2, 1918 *Flushing Daily Times* reported he was missing in action, and had probably been killed. [7] One can only imagine the anguish suffered by the Bigler parents having confirmed the loss of one son, and now - possibly two. To their great relief, a subsequent report indicated he had returned to duty. [8] It was later learned he had been held for a time in an unidentified German Prisoner of War camp.[9] His return to America's shores was delayed until May 1919, whereupon he was officailly discharged from the army. [10]

Jacob Bigler Sr., whose German-born father had brought his family to College Point after the Civil War, passed away in January 1927. His wife Mary, who was also born in Germany, would become active in the Oscar Ammann Post, and die in November 1945.

22

The Lord Was With Me

Local newspapers reported war news in every issue in the final weeks of September through the end of November. On the same day headlines proclaimed big gains in France, it was reported that John W. Rapp's Empire Art Metal Company had acquired another building in which to manufacture shells. [1] In addition to building submarine chasers, the College Point Boat Company was now constructing pontoons, barges, and flying boats, as well as canvas sails, and life jackets. [2] Perhaps the most engaging announcement came from an umbrella group of village clubs and leaders laying out plans for a mid-September carnival and block party. The three-day, weekend event would feature jazz bands, lively music, dancing, glee club performances, and vaudeville singers each night. Under the auspices of the Knights of Columbus, the gala was designed to offer lots of opportunities for enjoyment, all to benefit the village's Soldiers' and Sailors' Fund. [3] With more than two thousand people in attendance, when it closed the carnival was deemed a great success. [4]

Simultaneously, the leaders for College Point's Fourth Liberty Loan drive expressed hope that the canvassers would uphold the good record the town had made in the previous three. [5] In June, fifteen months earlier, the government had decided to put out its first issue of bonds for carrying on the war. With no organization in place, the village's Scoutmasters and Boy Scouts stepped into the breach, securing bond subscriptions amounting to more than $37,000. The second and third were even more successful. For the latter, an executive committee made up of prominent residents, a

who's who of sorts, was formed. Their task was to go door-to-door soliciting the community's support. They were successful beyond imagination,
exceeding a quota of $131,000 by almost 28%, or $347,000. [6] What was
even more newsworthy, according to one report, was that the money had
been secured largely from Americans of German descent, [7] as if the community could or would have done otherwise had their ancestry been otherwise. College Point families were not only paying with their pocketbooks at
home, some were paying with the blood of husbands, and sons in France.
Bad news traveled slowly, but not the flow of men being sent to Camp
Upton and other training facilities.

Letters were published frequently. In one written by College Pointer
William Hoenig, he told of his best friend, and their first time together
in battle against the Germans. The soldier related how he had escaped
unscathed, while his friend, at his side, was killed. [8] Hoenig mourned his
loss; William Jockers lamented that he would not be going off to war. Just
one week after a very enthusiastic crowd had turned out to cheer on a
group of inductees departing for Camp Gordon, Jockers among them,
camp officials rejected him. "Chuck", as he was called, stood less than five
feet tall, and was very light weight. Though he tried hard to get into some
department of the service, all attempts were thwarted. He came back to
College Point a very disappointed young man. [9] Similarly, Corporal Robert
Rausch, who had enlisted before the first draft, wrote dejectedly from Eagle
Pass, Texas. Soon after entering the army he was sent to Mexico to guard
the border. The return address on the envelope read, 'No Man's Land', but
that name seems to fit Eagle Pass, he wrote. "When I volunteered for the
army, I thought I would see foreign service in a short time, but it seems it
was my misfortune to be sent into this desert." He was clearly disappointed
that the war had seemingly passed him by. [10]

Before the end of the year, the names of many stricken soldiers
would be published. William Thorogood was gassed, and Corporal Joseph
Soukup, shot in the left knee. Pvt. Martin Zwicke wrote his wife to tell her
he'd been wounded on October 15th. "I lay on my back on the battlefield
for an hour and a half, and every move I made, a German machine gun
from some house top would open up on me. I was caught in a German

barrage and all kinds of shells were dropping around me, gas shells too. I had a very close shave with death as I lay on the battlefield, but I had no fear as the Lord was with me." [11]

Privates Edward Doran, Charles Freygang, Jr., Walter E. J. Garvin, Manuel Hook, Raymond W. Jacob, Ernest Otto, Charles Ruckdaschel, Emil Schnell, and George Gray all suffered wounds, some more serious than others. Schnell described how he lay helpless in "No Man's Land" for seven hours before being rescued by the Red Cross. [12] In his letter written from "somewhere in France", the censor's now familiar phrase, George Gray could say only that he was recovering in a base hospital. [13] Private Jacob Bigler, whose brother August was already listed among the fallen, was reported listed as having been killed in action. [14]

Aware that a great many soldiers and sailors would be returning from the war handicapped by wounds so serious that they would be forced to enter new trades and industries, the Red Cross established an Institute for Crippled and Disabled Men in Manhattan. Thousands of factories, shops and offices across the country pledged to open their doors to the nation's wounded veterans upon their return. With the war still raging, John W. Rapp immediately hired a one-armed man, a "cripple" as they were termed, to work in his factory. At the same time the American Hard Rubber Company committed to setting aside fifty jobs for "cripples" recommended by the organization. [15] More than thirty men from College Point would suffer wounds, some slight and others severe. It is not known if any sought training at the Red Cross Institute.

For two days in September, the 25th and 26th, America suffered 124,000 battle casualties in an intense bombardment that had started on the 12th aimed at the St. Mihiel Salient, a triangular wedge of land in northeastern France. Unassailable since the fall of 1914, it had long been occupied, and heavily fortified by the Germans. Two weeks later, nearly seven thousand men were either killed or wounded in the Argonne Forest,[16] considered a "quiet area", and a place where troops were sent for rest periods. [17] From September 26th through the signing of the Armistice on November 11th, the Meuse-Argonne Offensive, as it was called, was the climax toward which the efforts of American Expeditionary Forces were directed since arrival of U.S. troops in France. Forty-seven days of relentless war making resulted in the loss of approximately forty-nine thousand men, the number representing 40% of America's total battlefield losses. [18]

"From time immemorial, the Argonne had proved a stumbling block to military operations. Julius Caesar went around it. Napoleon avoided it. In this war, neither Germans nor French,could push all the way through it." [19] It was dense, only seven miles wide by two miles deep, but from the war's earliest days neither the German nor Allied armies had been able to take it in its entirety.

The offensive began at dusk around 2:30 in the morning with a short though intense artillery barrage; a monstrous chorus of destruction [20] that expended more explosives in three hours than had been used in all of the American Civil War. To say "Argonne" to an American of the 1930's was akin to saying "Normandy" to his counterpart in the 1950's; bloodbaths in both instances. While it was the largest American operation in the First World War, the Argonne is little remembered today. [21]

The bombardment was followed at 5:30 by a planned rolling barrage, a tactic in which troops went over the top into no man's land, running in front of the fire of their own guns. Forward movement was steady with concealed machine gunners allowing the first lines to pass on unmolested then firing upon the second. The Boche gunners took aim and their deadly fire left behind the second unit's dead and wounded. It was this type of fighting that marked the entire Meuse-Argonne action. [22]

From late September on, casualty reports from battles fought at the St. Mihiel Salient, the Argonne Forest, and as the war ran down, the Hindenburg Line, which the Germans regarded as impregnable, were published. They were especially disheartening as horrific stories of wartime carnage filled the pages of the nation's newspapers. More and more telegrams arrived in big cities and small towns across America. "The Bureau regrets to inform you", they began, followed by the report that a loved-one had become a casualty of war, wounded or perhaps, as in so many instances, killed in action. Over the course of the offensive, the Argonne Forest broke down into pockets of small unit action, and it was during this period that nineteen men from College Point lost their lives, but not all in battle.

Reports that James J. Powers, Emil J. Schwab, Arthur B. Rooney, Christian Geidel, Louis Doerr, Ernest B. Plitt, Stephen M. Schwab, Edward J. Stack, Hyman Lashiwer, Louis Fritz, Benjamin Franklin Blue, Louis Schmidt, August Breisacher, John B. Endres, Thomas J. McCormick, Albert W. Frey, William J. N. Mohrmann, Henry Zimmer, and Arthur Kraemer had died in the service of their country would soon follow.

23

James Joseph Powers

August 3, 1871 - September 25, 1918

E arly in May 1917, recruiting posters for the 1st Reserve Engineers began appearing in locations all around New York City. Some probably made it to College Point, where James J. Powers saw one, prompting thought to the notion of enlisting. But why would a man well past his fortieth birthday, with a wife, and three grown children, consider joining the army, epecially in a time of war? The pay offered ranged from $25 to $75 per month, $425 to $1,300 in today's dollars. The national army being formed, needed men, no age limit stated, with a wide range of skills; enginemen, brakemen, carpenters and machinists, among others. [1] One role had special appeal for him, chauffeur. If there was anything Powers had done in his life, he had driven motorized vehicles.

Born in the city of Waterford, Ireland on August 3, 1871, he had come to America in 1889, and in 1895, met and married Bridget Josephine Power. Her maiden name was simply coincidence. Following the December 1896 birth of a son named James, [2] the Powers family returned to the United Kingdom. Two daughters were born while living abroad, Irene and Katharine.

Arriving back in the U.S. in June 1900, James and Josephine planned to settle in Whitestone, [3] but exactly where they lived, or for how long, is unknown. The 1910 census record shows the family living in Cambridge, Massachusetts. James was working as a chauffeur for a private family. It was there perhaps that the photograph of him wearing a touring cap and goggles, may have been taken.

The Powers family returned to College Point after 1915, where on May 19, 1917, James ventured to a recruiting office in Manhattan. There he began the enlistment process, lowering his age by thirteen years. [4] The enrolling officer did not ask, thus ten days later, James J. Powers found himself at Fort Totten in Company B of the 1st Reserve Engineers. The unit would soon be designated the Eleventh Engineers (Railway) to distinguish it from the 1st Engineers, National Army, and the 1st Engineers, Regular Army. [5]

Over the next two months, the regiment spent its time preparing for its eventual mission; to work alongside British in the maintenance and repair of existing French rail lines damaged by shelling and bombardment since the start of hostilities. Destined for railroad work, the engineers were also charged with constructing any and all new lines as necessary. If the war was to be won, the transportation of men and materials of war throughout France was going to be critical.

Time went by quickly. Private Powers had his rank upgraded to wagoner or wagon driver, and before long, the regiment embarked on a two-week sail to England. Following arrival, King George V and his wife Queen Mary, reviewed the regiment; truly an historic event. "For the first time in history, a British King reviewed a regiment of American soldiers, saluted the colors of the nation that 141 years before, had taken up arms against King George III, his great, great grandfather. In return, he received the salute of the regimental colors of the first volunteer regiment of American soldiers raised to participate in the World War." [6] One can only imagine what James J. Powers from Waterford might have felt at this time, he a son of Ireland fighting on the side of the British, some might say, his sworn enemy. There was much disdain on the part of a great many Irish-Americans when it came to cozying up with Great Britain. Whatever his sentiments or political beliefs, as a naturalized American citizen, he was committed to doing just that.

Throughout its time in France, the unit was engaged in one of its primary tasks, track maintenance. As anticipated, all the shelling had inflicted much damage on rail beds and bridges, thus the work of the regiment went on unceasingly. [7] The unit was continually on the move, and occasionally under fire, sometimes taking part as infantry. More tracks had to be repaired, and the work of transforming continued, as all lines had to be ready for service. It was heavy work, dirty work, seemingly endless work.

On September 25th, as the Argonne Offensive was about to begin, the Eleventh Engineers was given the order to construct a new line between the villages of Aubréville and Aprémont, a town northeast of the Argonne Forest. Before this could happen, it was necessary to get the first part of the line staked out. To this end, a survey party was sent out to Aubréville with Sergeant Powers acting as chauffeur. Depositing his passengers safely, he parked his vehicle at the side of the road to await their return. Powers had been there some time when at about 5:30 P.M. a shell struck in the road close to the car, near to where he was standing. It exploded, and Powers suffered severe wounds. Taken immediately to a nearby Mobile Hospital, he died there four hours later. His body was buried the next day in the military cemetery at Blerecourt. [8] According to hospital Chaplain John M. Louis who buried him, Powers had no tags, only a disk bearing his name on his wrist. It was nailed to the cross that marked his grave, number 32. [9]

Since her husband's enlistment, Josephine Powers had moved from College Point to Long Island City. As a result, she never received official notification of his death. She did, however, receive a letter dated September 29th from Private Edgar K. Hardy, a soldier who served alongside James. Hardy, however, was able to add no particulars as to how his James J.

Powers had died. Subsequently, the widow sent a request to Washington asking for more information. What she received in reply amounted only to confirmation of his death. [10] Josephine Powers probably never did learn the entire story.

In May 1919, a representative from the Adjutant General's office made contact. His letter indicated her husband's remains could be returned to the U.S. for burial at a national cemetery of her choosing. In a hand-written note, she replied, "I would prefer the body of Sgt. James J. Powers (my husband) remain in France as he received a Military Burial and a tombstone from his companions. I want to remember my husband as I last saw him. I know he is in Heaven." [11]

Following the war, his body was removed from the cemetery at Blerecourt and buried for a time in Grave 183, Section 99, Plot 4 at the Meuse-Argonne Military Cemetery. On October 5, 1921, his remains were disinterred then reburied the next day in Row 31, Block E, Grave 30 in the same cemetery. [12]

In 1930, Josephine Powers took part in the Pilgrimage for War Mothers and Widows, accepting the Government's offer to visit her husband's grave. At some point during the month-long journey, it is likely she and Paula Ammann, Oscar's mother, passed some time perhaps sharing memories of College Point. With Tommy Fagan having served in a Canadian unit, his mother would not have been invited, even though he was buried in France. By default, Josephine Powers and Paula Ammann were the only two College Point mothers to take part in the pilgrimage.

Bridget Josephine Powers never remarried. She died in 1951 the village of Smallwood, Sullivan County, New York.

24

Emil John Schwab

June 18, 1894 - September 25, 1918

E mil John Schwab was the first College Point man to surrender his life fighting in the Argonne Forest. He grew up in College Point, attended a local school, worshiped at St. Fidelis Church, and by age fifteen, was working at the American Hard Rubber Company. He was drafted on May 28, 1918. One month after arrival at Camp Meade, Maryland, about fifteen miles south of Baltimore, was assigned to Company K of the 316th Infantry. Serving alonside him were two other College Point men, Arthur Rooney and Charles Ruckdaschel. [1] Their time at the cantonment was brief, two weeks. On July 7th, bidding farewell to the Old Line State, Emil, Arthur and Charles went by ferry to Hoboken, and then on to France aboard the *Agamemnon*. [2] The vessel was formerly a liner with German registry, the *Kaiser Wilhelm II*. Before the war started, the ship built in 1903 by the North German Lloyd Steamship Company, had made regularly scheduled trips between Germany and New York. When war was formally declared, the government seized the vessel, gave her a new name, then transformed the steamer into a troopship. [3]

Departing in early July, the crossing took an uneventful nine days, save for the occasional anxiety brought on by the possibility that a submarine might launch a torpedo. Throughout the remainder of July, August, and September, intermittent training continued in France, as the 316th made its way east, arriving in mid-September in the area of Montfaucon. [4] Emil became acquainted with life in the trenches, not knowing how short a life that would be.

"On the night of September 24th, the 316th Infantry sent squads out in front of the lines to cut wide gaps in the barbed wire entanglements in front of the trenches. It was a sure sign a drive was about to take place. On the following day, tanks rumbled all day past the 316th's camp and heavy guns mounted on tractors were moved into position. Field Officers held meetings throughout the 25th, yet neither the day nor the hour of the attack, was announced. Nevertheless, the 316th eventually learned where it would be situated in the battle to come. [5]

If the information contained in Emil Schwab's burial file is correct, it is quite possible he was unaware of any of these events. The record states his death took place on September 25th, the day preceding the start of the Argonne Offensive. According to a 316th Regiment historian, Carl Edward Glock, he may have been one of the men sent out to cut barbed wire, perhaps cut down by a sniper's bullet or random shellfire. Such things happened. However it occurred, the circumstances under which he died, are not a part of his file. Formal notification of his death was sent via telegram to his mother, Dora Getzelman Schwab. They were followed by the requisite communications regarding the return of his body to the U.S. Following his death, Emil John Schwab was buried in the Meuse Argonne Cemetery #1232 at Romagne sous-Montfaucon in Meuse, France. [6]

The U.S. Army transport *Cambrai* arrived in Brooklyn carrying the rermains of soldiers who had died during the war, one of them Emil Schwab. [7] C. Johann & Sons brought his casket to College Point where a memorial Mass was celebrated at St. Fidelis. Burial followed in St. Mary's Cemetery in Flushing. [8] In December 1925, his younger brother Ferdinand applied for, and the Veterans' Administration approved, a headstone to be placed at his grave in commemoration of his military service. [9]

Dora Schwab passed away in 1944. She was buried in Mt. St. Mary's Cemetery in Flushing, where in 1913, she had buried Emil's father, Ferdinand.

25

Arthur Bartholomew Rooney

March 16, 1889 - September 26, 1918

If they did not know each other prior to May 28, 1918, the day they were drafted, Arthur Rooney and Emil Schwab undoubtedly shared a great many experiences between that day, and September 25th, four months hence. Fifteen months earlier, on registration day, Rooney was working as a street cleaner for the City of New York, while Schwab was toiling at the American Hard Rubber Company. It is quite possible, and more than likely their paths did not cross until the day they left together on a train bound for Camp Upton. Charles Ruckdaschel completed the trio, all assigned to Company K, 316th Infantry. [1]

Based on census and other records going back to the mid-19th century, Arthur Rooney's heritage was a combination of English heritage, his father, James, and Irish, his mother, Agnes. James Rooney was a post-Civil

War army veteran stationed at Fort Custer in Montana, a few years after the infamous Battle of the Little Bighorn. Although born on the day before the feast of St. Patrick, and by virture of his surname, it might be presumed Arthur was raised Roman Catholic. That would be wrong. His religious affiliation was Church of England; his family attended the Episcopal Church of St. Paul in College Point.

Rooney, Schwab and Ruckdaschel took part in the short-lived training offered at Camp Meade. They sailed together to France aboard the *Agamemnon*, and then traveled the rails east to the front. Schwab was killed on the 25th. On the next day, September 26th, the first day of the Meuse-Argonne Offensive, Arthur Rooney lost his life.

The offensive began at a very early hour with a brief, yet fierce, artillery bombardment. Three hours later, troops were supposed to join the attack behind a planned rolling barrage. By that time, the 316th was on the roads groping it's way forward, faintly conscious of the immensity of the struggle about to open; its ultimate objective the impregnable fortress stronghold at Montfaucon.

This was the first time these men had been in front of the fire of their own guns, the rolling barrage. At 5:30, the first troops went over the top into no man's land. The German guns opened up, and the 316th stepped out into its first real baptism of fire. Forward movement was steady, but unwittingly, the regiment had passed a number of concealed machinegun nests. The Boche gunners took aim, and their deadly fire left behind the unit's first dead and wounded. It was this type of fighting that marked the entire Meuse-Argonne action. Concealed machine gunners allowed the first lines to pass on unmolested, then fired upon the second. [2] This is very likely the manner in which Arthur Rooney died, and for both he and Emil Schwab, their first day in battle would also be their last.

Because the Argonne Offensive took place over more than a week's time, Arthur's body was not recovered until the second day of October. Agnes Rooney's first request for its return to the U.S. was made in early February 1919. One month later she asked for his photograph if one was available. There is no indication that a copy was ever sent. Originally interred in the Montfaucon Cemetery, his remains were subsequently moved to the Argonne American Cemetery in the village of Romagne. On St. Patrick's Day, 1921, Agnes petitioned once again to have her son's body returned to College Point for burial. [3] In mid-June, his remains began a homeward-bound journey aboard the U.S. Army transport *Cantigny*, arriving at Hoboken in early August. [4] Funeral Director C. Johann and Sons fulfilled its necessary role and St. Paul's rector, Rev. Benjamin Mottram, led the services. [5] A firing squad from Fort Totten, and a large delegation from the Oscar Ammann American Legion Post, accompanied the cortege to Brooklyn's Greenwood Cemetery. Arthur's remains were buried there with full military honors. [6]

Schwab, Rooney and Ruckdaschel undoubtedly got to know one another very well, but only Ruckdaschel, although shot in the head during the same Argonne offensive, [7] recovered and returned to College Point.[8] Agnes Rooney lived on into her late 80's, dying in January 1942, in College Point.

26

Christian Geidel

December 19, 1889 - September 26, 1918

C hristian Geidel was named after his grandfather who came to America from Germany in the late 1840's. His was one of the first families to settle in College Point after Conrad Poppenhusen built his rubber factory. He was numbered among the village's numerous tailors with a large family, three sons and three daughters. Frederick, born in 1862, was the second son and second child, who grew up in the shadow of his first-born, older brother, Christian. He was a celebrated baseball player for the College Point Hayrakers in 1886. In that year, the team won most of its games, and at the end of the season, traveled to Scranton, Pennsylvania where they won a championship. [1] According to newspaper reports, Christian Geidel excelled as the team's catcher. He had all the requisite tools. He could hit well, and was also a good base runner. [2] By September, Geidel's thirty year-old baseball exploits were distant, but not forgotten memories, as Frederick's son, with the same first name, prepared to go to war.

As had many of the men who registered on June 5th, Christian was a graduate of Public School No. 27, and worked at the American Hard Rubber Company. [3] Come the end of that summer, on the night before leaving for Camp Upton, he and Alfred Stengel were given a celebrational send-off. [4] Both men were assigned to infantry regiments. Alfred went to the 307th, and Christian to the 305th, Company B. [5] The following April, Christian was on a troop ship in a zigzagging convoy making its way to Liverpool. Instead of undergoing additional training in England, he found himself, and his regiment, on a train to Dover, followed by another water-borne voyage, this one across the Channel. The sky was gray and the wind was bitter cold. There was to be no training in England after all. [6]

Over the months to come, the 305th traveled across France arriving at the Argonne Forest in late September. In the pre-dawn hours of the 26th, a massive offensive commenced with a rolling artillery barrage. As the 305th advanced, what Geidel might have seen before him was a wooded series of steep valleys and ridges, once heavily forested land. It was now barren, marked by numerous trenches and wire systems, a twisted and tortuous maze of earthworks, caverns, pits, dugouts, gun emplacements and barriers; outposts that were scarcely more than shell-holes. "No Man's Land" and German trenches, had been turned into a series of craters by the heavy concentration of artillery. All was desolation. The barbed wire had not been cut, and any advances to be made, would come with much difficulty. [7]

Perhaps on any other day, ground troops might have followed the barrage at a normal rate. Little did they expect to find such a network of deep trenches with their multitude of dugouts. Nor did they ever believe that there could possibly be such a dense tangle of barbed wire. With the exception of the wire, the trees and the trenches, practically no opposition was encountered going through the front lines. [8]

Throughout the course of that day, an advance of a little more than a mile was made, and "in the afternoon while lying in a funk hole in the denuded Argonne Forest on a hillside, Christian Geidel was killed by enemy artillery fire. He was hit and died shortly afterward before treatment could reach him. The next day he was buried along with three comrades who died at the same time, from the same cause. [9]

Episcopalian chaplain Rev. Duncan H. Browne, before the war Pastor of Christ Church on Staten Island, buried him and his three comrades in arms. He made certain that a cross marked Christian's grave, and his identification tag was buried with him. For his numerous heroic efforts on this first day of battle, Browne was awarded the nation's second highest military honor, the Silver Star, [10] earning, at the same time, the nickname, "the Fighting Parson of the 105th. [11]

On October 17th, Anna and Fred Geidel received word from the War Department that their son had been killed. [12] Christmas was passed in sorrow, and three more years would go by before their son's remains would be returned to the United States. At the army's request, undertaker C. Johann and Sons called for his body at Hoboken on Monday, October 10th. [13]

Overcoats and sweaters were called for two days later, and conditions were not at all ideal for playing baseball. Cloudy and cold at the Polo Grounds, the National League's New York Giants team was getting ready to play the American League's pennant winner, the New York Yankees. It was game seven of the World Series. [14] Former Haymaker star Christian Geidel, was probably interested in the game's outcome, and for the first time in history, he would be able to listen to it on the radio. [15] Instead, he was at Flushing Cemetery taking part in the funeral service for his nephew, conducted by Rev. Benjamin Mottram.

In the too-often repeated ritual, members of Oscar Ammann Post 853 accompanied the cortege to Flushing Cemetery. Anna, in the company of her two surviving sons, Alfred and Walter, buried Christian with full military honors. [16] On a cold December 16th two years earlier, she had buried her husband Fred in the same plot. [17] Born in 1901, Walter was too young to have served, but Alfred, born in 1895, did. He was drafted in May 1918, but with one son already serving in France, Anna Geidel was probably very happy to learn that this son was assigned to the 22nd Infantry, a unit not sent overseas. Its duty was to guard the docks at Hoboken against possible saboteurs and spies. Fred became a butcher after the war, and when his country called again in April 1942, Alfred registered. He died sixteen months later. Anna Geidel lived on until August 1947, and only Walter lived longer. He passed away in October 1983. All are buried in Flushing Cemetery.

27

Louis Bismarck Doerr

May 10, 1892 - September 26, 1918

Every College Point merchant marine, sailor or soldier who died in the service of his country, was mourned by relatives, friends and the community at large; none more than Louis Bismarck Doerr. He very likely got his middle name in honor of Otto Von Bismarck, a late 19th Century German statesman who in 1871, became the first Chancellor of the German Empire.

Louis was born in Perth Amboy, New Jersey, the third of six children. Some time after his birth, German émigrés William and Marie Doerr moved their growing family to the Krischerville section of Staten Island, and then to College Point. Louis, or "Lolly" as family and friends called him, attended P.S. 27 and, after graduation, continued his education at the Poppenhusen Institute. [1]

From the earliest days of his youth, Lolly was an excellent athlete. When an 8th grade student, he played second base on the school's 1906 Queens Borough Public School Championship baseball team. Had they defeated the Brooklyn school they faced, they would have been all-city champs. In recognition of their achievement, each team member received a medal, and in words of encouragment were told, "If you must lose, and all have to suffer defeat sometime, then let it happen only after all your best powers have been put forth." [2]

School Principal Henry Delamain.
Top row Left to right: Charles Martini, George Washington Henrich, Herman Holm, Thomas Sheridan, Manuel Hook, Daniel Frank, coach. Second row: Rudolph Kussman. Bottom row; Charles Schreiner, John Gerhardt. Louis Doerr, Gordon Wood.

Four years later, Louis was working as a printer at American Hard Rubber Company, playing on its baseball and football teams. Though born and raised a Lutheran, he also starred on St. Fidelis Catholic Lyceum squads, and would soon add bowling to his repertoire. In Germany, it was called kegling, so in College Point it was a popular pastime. Louis excelled.

On June 5, 1917, he was working as a special patrolman for the New York City Harbor Police, serving as a reserve to fill the place of a man in the service. [3] After passing his physical, he was certified for military service. On September 29th, he was inducted and sent to Camp Upton where he became a member of Company F, 302nd Engineers. His brother Fred, older by seven months, was also drafted, and soon joined him in the 302nd. He was assigned to Company E. [4] In February, Louis made Sergeant; Fred became a Corporal. [5]

There was training to be sure, but not all of their time was spent on military matters. The 302nd fielded a very good football team, and because Doerr had been a standout at that sport, he won a spot. The team was very good, in fact the best in the entire 77th Division. They beat all challenges and experienced intra-regimental defeat only once, a return match against the 306th Infantry, a team they had previously bested. In the middle of the night of March 28th, the 302nd Engineers boarded the *RMS Carmania*, sailed for Liverpool, then continued on to France. [6]

Three months later, Company F was billeted in the French city of Baccarat, near the border of Switzerland. The unit was engaged in engineer work, repairing roads, planning and building new trenches and dugouts, mining bridges, and putting up barbed wire; all things necessary for the conduct of war. [7] But all was not work. Lolly took time to write home to tell his parents of an interesting experience he had while playing baseball. "We played a game the other day and in the fifth inning we stopped playing because Fritz started out to play one of his nasty little tricks with his airplanes. We had an air raid, which lasted an hour. Last week we played a good game and we won it. I got two three-baggers, two two-baggers and a home run." He also let on that the team was soon to leave for Paris to play, and acknowledged having received five letters - all at the same time. "You don't know how good it makes a fellow feel to receive a letter from someone so far away." [8]

September found the Regiment on the move eastward, its destination, the Argonne Forest. Between the 20th and the 26th, little or no work was done by day, for fear the Germans might discover that the Americans had arrived in force, and would then suspect an attack was to be made. The night, however, told a different story. Since the area was heavily fortified with barbed wired, much of the dark time was spent cutting it away. This was done to facilitate troop movements when the battle commenced. Zero hour came at 5:30 on the morning of the 26th. It was preceded by a monstrous French artillery barrage, soon taken up by the American artillery. Out of the trenches and over the top went the troops, but due to a very heavy fog, there was scarcely any return fire by the Germans. Everywhere, it seemed, the enemy trenches were deserted. The men of Company F advanced with the attacking infantry, their job to explore enemy dugouts, mark trails, and perform whatever engineering work was required. [9]

On this first day, Louis's platoon became lost, and got ahead of the advancing Infantry. The detachment encountered a party of German machine gun snipers whom they promptly engaged. [10] In the course of mopping up, Private Louis Doerr was instantly killed by shell fire, while acting as a guard over seven German prisoners taken. This was in the Argonne Forest near La Harazée." [11]

Upon hearing the news, John G. Embree of the College Point Red Cross, whose son Harold had been killed in action at the end of July, cabled the American Red Cross requesting any additional information that might be available. [12] There was no reported response.

Days after his death, Louis' Commanding Officer, Captain Robert C. O'Donnell, penned a letter to William Doerr. "It is with extreme regret that I have to report the death of your son on September 26, 1918. He was one of a party bringing in several German prisoners, when the enemy suddenly pounded the party with shellfire. Instead of seeking cover himself, with great presence of mind, he courageously kept the prisoners in line, getting them safely into shelter. Three had already passed into the dugout when a shell burst, killing him, and two of the prisoners, instantly. Louis was found with them at the entrance of the dugout, his rifle with bayonet fixed, still grasped in his hands, proving that he had been faithful to his duties to the end. [13]

His comrades brought him in and he was carefully laid in a casket, buried in a little French Cemetery, and given an impressive military funeral under the direction of the Regimental Chaplain. Earlier in the day, he was one of the party who courageously volunteered to enter a ravine strongly held by the enemy to search for a missing comrade. Your son was one of the best of men in the Company". [14] His words bring to mind those spoken at the awards ceremony in 1906, "If you must lose, and all have to suffer defeat sometime, then let it happen only after all your best powers have been put forth. [15]

Enclosed in a rustic fence, Louis' grave at La Harazée lay undisturbed until early summer 1921. Disinterred in June, his remains were returned to America aboard the U.S. Armry transport *Wheaton* arriving at Hoboken in late August. [16] C. Johann and Sons brought his coffin to the family home,[16] and on September 2nd, members of the Oscar Ammann Post convened there to conduct Legion funeral services. The village's Marvin Glee Club sang hymns. [17] The next day, to honor their fallen comrade, the "Boys of the Point" placed Lolly's portrait in the center of a large and beautiful floral piece, fully five feet in circumference. [18] To them, Louis Doerr was the same man in civilian life when it was that his great reservoir of energy was expended in play, instead of the grim business of war. The crowds went wild over him. Whenever a crucial point was reached in a contest, it was always Louis Doerr who pulled his team through. [19]

Four of his teammates from P.S. 27 entered military service; John Gerhart, George Washington Henrich, Manuel Hook and Charles Schreiner. Gerhart was in the 306th Infantry, and a number of other units. Schreiner never went overseas. Henrich, born February 22, 1891 thus explaining the origin of his name, served in the Navy's Quartermaster Corps. Hook came home from France after being severely wounded on October 17, 1918. He had served in Company C, 102nd Field Signal Battalion. [20]

Hundreds of friends and comrades attended Louis' funeral, as did his Captain, Robert C. O'Donnell. The cortege included more than fifty members of the Independent Order of Red Men, of which Louis had been a member. Behind them came the firing squad followed by three of his comrades carrying the floral piece. William Baumert, mistakenly reported as having been killed in action, represented the army, Charles Simon, the Navy, and Harvey Lee, the Marines. More than forty automobiles followed the hearse, and many others had preceded the procession to Flushing Cemetery. There Louis Doerr was laid to rest with full military honors. Lutheran graveside services conducted by Rev. Arthur Halfmann of St. John's, were impressive, and the sound of taps was particularly touching. As one bugler, perhaps Edward Martin, blew the last note of the call, another in the distance echoed it. [21] The story is told that when his burial was taking place, someone asked his mother how she could be sure the body in the sealed coffin was that of her son? She replied, "Well then I'm burying someone's son. Perhaps someone will bury my son." [22]

Rev. Halfmann's day at Flushing Cemetery was only half over. Later in the afternoon, he would preside at the funeral service for John H. Gerlach, whose loose-leaf binding company had provided jobs for many young men from the village. [23]

The family remained in College Point. Marie Doerr lived on until her death in 1927. William lived six years longer. Both are buried in Flushing Cemetery with Louis. Fred Doerr passed away on May 9, 1965, and is buried in Long Island National Cemetery. Another brother Killian called "Killy" by everyone, died in January 1972. Lolly's sister Regina married William Kaufman, Lolly's boyhood friend, as well as football and baseball teammate. A navy veteran, William contracted influenza around 1922, and in an effort to regain his health, spent time in a newly established camp for tubercular veterans in Tupper Lake, New York. Health improved, he was able to return to College Point, but in spring 1923 his condition again became serious, requiring a return to the camp. He died there on August 22, 1923. He was 27, [24] the same age as Lolly on the day he lost his life in the Argonne Forest. William Kaufman was buried in Flushing Cemetery.

28

Ernest B. Plitt

October 22, 1888 - September 28, 1918

Tennis was the sport pursued by Ernest B. Plitt. It was one at which he excelled, playing on the Elmhurst Tennis Club courts. His older brother Godfrey, and younger brother W. Irving also played. [1] Irving - the W stood for Washington - won the Long Island Tennis Club's Single's Championship in 1924. [2] He lost it a year later. [3] Tennis was not a big sport in College Point, though Harold Embree was a very good player. [4]

Ernest's grandfather George emigrated from Germany in the 1850's. For a brief time he made his home in Flushing, where a son, his namesake, was born. George Plitt, Jr. was Ernest's father. By 1860, the Plitt family was living in College Point, and in the decades that followed, George, Jr. rose to positions of prominence. At different times, he was the superintendent of one of the silk mills, and village postmaster.

Ernest was the sixth of seven children, and a 1904 graduate of P. S. 27.[5] Four years later, following his Flushing High School graduation, his family moved from College Point to the neighboring town of Elmhurst. He coninued playing tennis, but it appears his genuine interest lay elsewhere. At the time of his registration for the draft, he was working at Penn Station for the Long Island Railroad. [6]A few months later he was on his way to Camp Upton, assigned to Company H in the 306th Infantry. [7] There is no record of tennis being a contested sport.

On April 3rd, Ernie, as he was called, penned a letter to his brother Godfrey. "Just a few lines to let you know everything is O.K. I also want to take up a few things with you, which may seem a little foolish, but then you can never tell what will happen. Now as I told you, I have taken out the full $10,000 insurance. It's made out to mother and father should anything happen to me, and I want mother and father to have the payments while they are alive." He then went on to indicate how he wanted a number of personal items to be distributed adding, "That extra blanket I took from home I am going to try and take with me, for no doubt I will be able to make good use of it same as I have this winter. Am going to write the folks a note tonight so good night, with all my love, Ernie". [8] He had no idea of how prescient this letter was, nor the important role this missive would play.

Thirteen days later, Plitt, and four other College Point soldiers serving in the 306th, left for Europe. They were, Joseph Lauda, Harold Bennison, Frederick Stouke and Johan Bobst. Lauda would be wounded slightly, Bennison would be gassed and wounded severely, Stouke decorated for bravery, and only Bobst would come home physically unscathed. [9]

In the weeks and months that followed, the regiment made its way east, first crossing England by train, the Channel by boat, and then, by rail, through France. The regiment came under heavy shellfire for the first time on August 11th. Some men were wounded, and a few were killed This occurred near the villages of Mont Notre Dame and Basoches, where Russian-born Frederick Stouke, Company G did himself and his regiment proud.

With the American Forces in France, Correspondent Lincoln Eyre penned a piece in which he wrote, "Private Frederick Stouke is a German by origin, and one of the fighting men of the 306th Infantry, and what he did in the fierce local combats that have been raging behind the veil of smoke strangling the little town of Basoches from the outside world, forms a highly significant and encouraging commentary on the kind of soldiers in the American Expeditionary Forces.

Stouke was helping to mop up a corner of Basoches when he came upon four Boches. One showed fight, so Stouke downed him with a grenade. Then he started rear-ward with the other three. Suddenly there came a German counter attack. Stouke, whose German is a good as his English, ordered the trio of prisoners into a shell hole, and from the same hole helped to stop the advancing foe. One of the prisoners tried to escape, so Stouke shot him. With the remaining two, the enemy's onslaught having been disposed of, he again set out to the rear. A machine gun bullet killed one of them, and a moment later, the other was wounded. Stouke hoisted him upon his back and staggered along for a mile or so, to regimental headquarters. When he got there, his gas mask, tin hat and cartridge belt had been shot away; his uniform was in rags, but he was volubly informing his wounded prisoner of the prodigious licking awaiting the Kaiser and all his tribe. [10]

In addition to the Belgian Croix de Guerre for his heroic actions, Stouke was awarded the Silver Star, America's third highest military decoration. His citation read, Private Stouke distinguished himself by gallantry in action while serving with Company G. 306th Infantry, American Expeditionary Forces, in action near Bazoches, France, 27 August 1918, in guarding a prisoner under heavy machine gun fire all day and bringing him back to our lines under cover of darkness. [11]

On September 6th, two days after Ernest made Sergeant, [12] Harold Bennison was gassed, suffered serious leg wounds, and was hospitalized. [13] Three weeks later, the unit was in the area of the Argonne Forest preparing for the big offensive that was to follow, an offensive in which Ernest Bernard Plitt would not get to play a role. On September 25th, the day before the battle's commencement, Plitt was gassed and sent immediately to a hospital located 120 miles south of the forest in the village of Allerey. It was better equipped to handle cases such as his.

This Hospital Center could house over 20,000 patients. As the battle unfolded, trains arrived day and night from the Argonne Front. During the height of the offensive, in one twenty-four hour period, fifteen trains came in, filling all hospitals far above capacity, the casualties suffering everything from mustard gas to high explosive shell wounds. [14] A number of cases of influenza and pneumonia were received during late September and early October, together with many gassed cases who were very susceptible to respiratory infections. [15] Ernest Plitt was in this group, and in short order, he died. The official date written was September 28th; the official cause cited as pneumonia. [16]

A lingering question could be, was Ernest Plitt's pneumonia brought on by the gas, or was it possibly the result of the influenza virus that was wreaking havoc among the troops?

The chaplain buried him in Section I, Grave 31, in a little village cemetery, officially called A. E. F. Cemetery No. 84. It was also his job to keep a register of all burials and serial numbers of graves, and to inform relatives of their loss. The local French citizens took special care of the cemetery placing floral offerings on the graves, and giving painstaking attention to the surrounding areas; a testament to their reverent remembrance of the dead. [17]

The news of his death was printed in the local newspapers. All commented on how well- liked the soldier had been, and one saying that he "was one of the crack players of the Elmhurst Tennis Club." [18] In recognition of Ernest's atheltic prowess, immediately after the war, the United States Lawn Tennis Association placed his name among others in the Association's Service Roll, "preserved as a memorial to the patriotism and loyalty of the tennis players of the United States who served in the U.S. Army, Navy, Marine Corps, Red Cross, YMCA, Knights of Columbus and other organizations of mercy. [19]

The remains of Ernest B. Plitt were returned to America aboard the U.S. Army transport *Wheaton* arriving on February 10th. [20] His funeral service was held on February 21st at the home of his brother E. Alfred

Plitt, whose family had stayed in College Point. A firing squad and forty uniformed members of the Elmhurst American Legion Post, accompanied the cortgege to Flushing Cemetery, where Ernest was laid to rest. [21]

Frederick Stouke survived the war. He arrived home on April 25, 1919 aboard the *Mt. Vernon*. [22] Shortly thereafter on June 22nd, he married a girl named Anna Woessner, but their life together was short-lived. Less than a year later, Stouke took to his bed with bronchial pneumonia, (was it the flu?) and died on April 27th. He was buried in Flushing Cemetery.

Ernest's father, George Plitt, passed away in June 1929; his wife Selma in January 1935. She was eighty-four. The letter her son had written in April 1918 became his last will and testament, and was instrumental in settling his mother's estate. [23]

29

Stephen Melbourne Schwab

June 11, 1893 - September 29, 1918

S tephen M. Schwab was born in College Point. His parents were Sydney M. Schwab, born in Brooklyn just after the Civil War, and Ella Louise Grell, born in College Point in 1873. Hers was a privileged College Point lineage.

Frederick W. Grell was her father. Born in 1846, he came to America from Germany in 1852, and at age ten began working in Poppenhusen's factory. Over the ensuing decades he rose to increasing levels of responsibility culminating in his appointment as general superintendent of the American Hard Rubber Company. [1] Grell was also an accomplished musician. He composed the "Poppenhusen March" played during a celebration in 1871 in honor of the peace that ended the Franco-Prussian War. [2] He also served as President of the College Point Savings Bank. [3]

Ella grew up in this environment, and in 1892, married liquor salesman Sydney M. Schwab. Stephen was her first-born son, followed by two others, Clifton in 1895, and Lawrence in 1897. At the time Ella deserted her husband, leaving Stephen behind, neighbors referred to them as "a model married couple." [4] It was soon learned she had taken her two younger sons to Rhode Island. "My wife has always been of a roving and dissatisfied disposition," said Sydney. "I provided a comfortable home for her, but she was hard to please." [5] Upon her return to College Point, Ella reunited her offspring and went off to live with her parents.

Stephen was named to the P. S. 27 honor roll in February 1905.[6] That achievement was followed in May, when a "diminutive Stephen Schwab representing the College Point schools, was the hero of the Queens County Schools games held at Donnelly's Grove. As principal runner for his school, he knew that a great deal depended on his performance. He badly sprained his ankle in the 100-yard dash, and was attended by local physician, Dr. J. D. McPherson. With his lame foot, Schwab went on to win the broad jump, and it was his fine running in the 440-yard relay that won that event for his school." [7] One month later, his mother married a surgeon, Dr. John A. MacIssac, a Roman Catholic,. She then took her three sons to live with her in Manhattan. After graduating from St. Agnes High School, [8] not to be confused with the Catholic school in College Point having the same name, Stephen enlisted in the National Guard, 7th Infantry. He was assigned to Company E in the spring of 1912. [9] Two years later, and one month after the start of the war, Stephen and Clifton sailed for Europe as Red Cross volunteers.[10] Upon return, Stephen served on the Mexican Border, where he made Sergeant. [11]

Shortly after America's entry into the war, he was mustered into the National Army being formed to fight Jerry, the Boche, the Heinies and the Huns. It is unlikely he gave any thought to his father, born to a German mother and probably bilingual, or to his own mother's one hundred percent German heritage. He was first and foremost an American, and a soldier.

Commissioned a 2nd Lieutenant and sent to Fort Wadsworth in Spartanburg, Schwab was considered, "without exception, the best of the younger officers of the regiment." [12] He was also its first casualty. While taking a special course in bayonet work, he had jumped, bayonet in hand, into a six-foot deep trench after a charge through barbed wire. As a result, he turned his ankle and broke his leg. [13] It was an accident that put him out of action for a considerable length of time.

Stephen was raised to 1st Lieutentant on the same day his unit departed for Europe, but due to an outbreak of measles, he was unable to accompany E Company across the Atlantic. [14] When restored to health and able to rejoin the regiment, it was already engaged in the war, and taking part in battles fought in both Belgium and France. In the former, College Point soldier Lawrence B. Trimble of Company K, was severely wounded. Just hours after the telegram bearing the news arrived, his mother received a letter from him. "I'm in excellent health, he said, and enjoying the game of chasing the Huns." [15] As if getting wounded once wasn't bad enough, after his return to action, Trimble was gassed, and then wounded once again the very next day. Another College Point man, H Company's Emil Boehm, also suffered serious wounds. [16] These two soldiers, along with other College Pointers, had been in training with Schwab at Spartanburg.

In late September, the men of E Company were entrenched in front of Mount Kemmel, the German's most famous observation post. It was described as "a huge, bare, bleak earthen mound bereft of bushes or trees. Battered and banged, it had been the target of artillery for years, as had been no other in France. [17] It was here during the earlier month of August that Lieutenant Schwab distinguished himself for his daring and fearlessness, and where, at the end of this September, that he would die.

On the 27th, the company moved up to the front lines. Rations were issued the next day, along with necessary equipment for the moment they would go over the top. They would try to do what other Allied armies had failed to do, break the Hindenburg Line, the most formidable defense system the Germans had constructed during the entire war. It was one of the strongest fortified positions ever known in military history. [18]

In the early morning hours of the 29th, the Germans began their own serious artillery assault, aware as they were, an attack was coming. Company E exited the trenches and began making the advance. Up over the top went the soldiers immediately met by machine gun bullets, and explosions all around. Exploding shells took their toll, and men fell by the score. One of the first was Lieutenant Benjamin T. Hammond, who had served on the Mexican border with Schwab. When Hammond fell, followed by the Company Captain, Harry Hayward, Stephen Schwab promptly took command. As he and a few other men from the unit set about binding Hammond's wounds, he himself was wounded in the jaw, fatally it turned out. All three men died. Company E had entered the fight with 170 men, but three days later retired from the line with only forty-six. It had been a costly three days. [19]

The final actions of Stephen Melbourne Schwab's life were anything but diminutive, and for them he was awarded a Divisional Citation in Special Order #86, "For fearlessness, skill, good judgment and determination manifested during his entire active service, and for courage in battle on September 29, 1918, during the attack of the Hindenburg Line, when he effectively held his position under heavy enemy fire until killed. [20]

Just a few days prior to learning of her son's death, Ella MacIsaac had received a letter in which he told her he had been recently decorated with the French Croix de Guerre for bravery in action. [21] All of this information she undoubtedly shared with Clifton, who had joined the 7th New York in 1914, but did not go overseas, and with Lawrence, who had enlisted in the Navy in April, 1917. [22]

After the war, Stephen's remains were disinterred then reburied in Plot D, Row 5, Grave 110 at the American Military Cemetery in Bony, France, In the pocket of his pants on the day he died were three dime-size French silver coins worth 50 Centimes each. They were buried with him. Divorced, remarried and living in Boston in 1930, Ella declined the government's offer to take part in the Mothers' Pilgrimage. [23] She died in January 1946 in Palm Beach, Florida. Clifton predeceased her dying in March 1928, one week before his brother's coffin was disinterred, then reburied a second time in Grave 9, Plot A, Row 28. [24] Lawrence passed away in 1978.

30

Edward J. Stack

May 18, 1897 - September 29, 1918

I t is unlikely Edward Stack ever knew Stephen Schwab before their time together in the army. They were separated by four years in age, and whereas Stephen attended P.S. 27, Stack very likely had studied at St. Fidelis School. Plus, Schwab was gone by summer, 1905.

Edward's parents were James Stack and his wife Dorothy, but friends and family called her Dora. Her maiden name was Pickel. Both were New York City-born, James to Irish immigrants. Dora had roots in Germany. Both had grown up in the village, next-door neighbors on Pickel and Stack Street, as it was called by the locals. [1]

They married in 1895 and raised ten children, six boys and four girls. Edward was their second child, working at a rubber factory when war was declared. Taking matters into their own hands, one week before the mandatory draft registration day, Edward and his younger brother Charles took themselves to the Flushing Armory. There they joined Company I of the 10th Regiment of the New York National Guard. Charles was transferred to a Wagon Company that never saw service overseas. Edward's experience was different. He went to Camp Wadsworth in Spartanburg, along with a number of other College Point men also transferred into the 107th. They were, Robert Banker, Emil Boehm, Henry Dono, William Hoenig, Edward O'Rourke, William Pauly, Lawrence Trimble and Stephen Schwab.

All participated in various sporting events and intra-company rivalries. On at least one occasion, they took in a play, a Broadway-bound musical comedy titled, *"You Know Me, Al."* What might have made it special for Stack, and the others was the presence on stage of one of their own, William Cyril Pauly, though not easily recognized. He was playing an appropriately clad, and elegantly made-up, chorus girl. [2] When Conrad Poppenhusen brought his comb-making factory to College Point in 1854, Pauly's grandfather was one of the industrialist's most valued employees. Also named William, the elder Pauly held a number of comb-related patents, and in time became superintendent of the factory [3] that employed more than fifty men and boys who went to war between 1917 and 1918.

There was light drizzle throughout the 28th of September, a day the 107th spent getting as much rest as possible preparing for the battle about to begin. On this day, Father Peter Hoey, the 107th's Catholic Chaplain, set up a little altar and celebrated Mass. More than a thousand men 'received the Savior's most precious gift,' and those who later perished in the fight, "died with the Blood of Jesus still fresh upon their lips." [4] Edward Stack, a member of the St. Fidelis Lyceum, was very likely among the communicants. Had his parents and family been told this information, it might have provided them some small comfort.

The next day's objective was to break the heavily fortified, and well-defended Hindenburg Line. Company I was specifically tasked with driving the Germans from an area bordered by a farm, the Guillemont Farm to the north, and a hill called the Knoll, to the south. The orders to move came at about 4:30 early in the morning of the 29th. Nearing the six o'clock hour, 140 men from Company I, Stack among them, were in the first units to go over the top. They were headed in the direction of the heavily fortified farm looking down the barrels of many German machine-gun batteries. Fifteen tanks from the American 301st American Tank Battalion preceded them ripping apart belts of barbed wire barriers some as high as nine feet, and opening gaps through which the soldiers were able to advance. But the tanks very shortly ran into trouble in the form of unmapped and forgotten British mines. Before the fifteen tanks covered 500 yards, all but one had been smashed. 'Blooey' they went, up in the air. [5]

With the tanks disabled and out of action and their own creeping artillery support landing about a thousand yards in front of them, the men of Company I kept moving forward at a measured pace set upon by enfilading machine-gun fire often engaging in desperate hand-to-hand combat while aeorplanes droned above occasionally dropping bombs on German trenches. If it wasn't bombs, it was gas and if it wasn't gas it was grenades and if it wasn't grenades it was the unceasing and withering machine-gun fire - heroism and heroics everywhere.

As the advance progressed to Guillemont Farm and the Knoll, other forces charged with mopping up, making certain no enemy combatants remained in the recently gained ground, failed to accomplish their most important and essential task. As Germans popped out of the ground from their secret tunnels, the Americans were caught from behind; Machine-gun fire flew in every direction raking the men of the 107th resulting in a great many casualties. " [6]

It was at this point in the eventually successful Battle of the Hindenburg Line that Edward Stack drew his last breath. The exact time and specific circumstances are unknown. He had been a Corporal a mere two weeks. [7]

Writing home to his parents in College Point, Charles Blaeser, an original Company I, 10th Regiment soldier serving in the 105th Infantry, told how he had helped to bury his uniformed comrade Corporal Edward J. Stack in the cemetery at Bony, a week and a day following his death. He also told of granting the request of a badly wounded German soldier. "I asked him what he wanted, and he told me a drink of water. I gave him a drink from my canteen and then he told me to look under his shirt, and showed me a shrapnel wound. He started to cry and I felt sorry for him. He said, "Comrade, shoot me", and he pointed to his head. Mother, I took my pistol and did my duty." [8] The fallen German soldier's request, undoubtedly spoken in his native tongue, was clearly understood by the doughboy, bilingual as so many were.

Of the 140 men from Company I who went over the top on September 29, 1918, twenty were all that survived, [9] unimaginable losses. In the ten months passed there, the unit sustained 1,918 casualties, 1,383 wounded, 437 deaths, and 98, who later died of their wounds. [10]

Following his battlefield death, Corporal Edward J. Stack was post-humously cited in orders, having performed in battle in a manner deemed worthy of the recognition by Major General O'Ryan, Commanding Officer, 27th Division. The citation reads, "For great courage and deter-mination in action. This soldier, in the face of terrific enemy machine gun fire, which inflicted heavy casualties on his company, pushed forward with great resolution through the enemy wire in front of Willow Trench and into the enemy trench. This in the battle of the Hindenburg Line, near Bony, France, September 29, 1918." [11]

His grave, marked by a cross, was located in the Military Cemetery at Bony until early April 1921, when his remains were returned to the house on Pickel Alley and Stack Street. There College Point service men assem-bled to pay their last respects. [12] At St. Fidelis Church, Pastor Ambrose Schumack celebrated a Solemn Requiem Mass for the repose of his soul. Burial followed in the very large Stack family plot at St. Mary's Cemetery in Flushing.

In early March 1919, William Hoenig, Edward O'Rourke, Robert Banker Emil Boehm, Henry Dono, and Lawrence Trimble returned safely to College Point. [13] So too did William Pauly, who was also cited for mer-itorious service, courage and devotion to duty in administering aid to the wounded in first aid stations and casualty clearing stations, during the operations of the division in France. [14] Pauly rounded out his career not as a dancer on the stage, but as a Private in the U.S. Army's 152nd Depot

Brigade,[15] its most famous member being Irving (*Oh How I Hate to Get Up in the Morning*) Berlin, he who served, but never went to France.

31

Hyman Lashiwer

March 1897 - October 4, 1918

Hyman Lashiwer's Military Record says that he was born in Odessa on the coast of the Black Sea in Russia, in March 1897. He was actually born about seventy miles northeast of the city in the village of Tulchin in what is today's Ukraine. The family was Jewish. Chaim Laschewer, as it appeared on the *SS Finland* manifest, came to America in the fall of 1913. His married brother Mojsche, Anglicized to Morris, probably met him at the pier. He had come to America in 1907 and was living in Brooklyn working toward making enough money to bring his wife Taube, and daughter Molly, to the U.S. They arrived in 1909, and were followed a year later by his and Hyman's sister, Eva. In September 1914, she married Barnet Kessler, another Russian émigré. The couple settled in Collge Point. According to the 1915 cenus, both were working at the American Hard Rubber Company.

June 2nd fell on a Saturday in 1917, and on that drizzly, chilly overcast day, Hyman, engaged in the wholesale fruit business in Manhattan, joined the United States Army. [1] A post-war article said he was living with Eva in College Point, but the address he provided was 90 Ridge Street, just off the approach to the Williamsburg Bridge in lower Manhattan. [2] It was called the "Jew's Bridge." When it opened in 1902, many of the Jewish settlers from the overcrowded Lower East Side began to cross it in order to relocate in the Williamsburg section of Brooklyn.

On the requisite forms he named his sister, Eva Kessler, as the person to contact in the event of an emergency. [3] He then started life in the Army at Fort Slocum, given Serial Number 40,917, and assigned to the 21st Recruit Company. Transferred, he spent the rest of his military career in Company M, 9th Infantry. [4]

His unit deployed to France in mid-September. Shipping out with him aboard the *SS Carmania*, was another young man from College Point named Joseph Fidelis Becker, assigned to Company A. In the middle of July the following year, Becker would be reported missing in action. [5] Much as Lashiwer had done, Becker had not waited to be drafted, enlisting shortly after Hyman. [6]

While Becker came home, Lashiwer's army career ended on October 4th, when he died of wounds received in action on September 12th, the opening day of the Battle of St. Mihiel. This was the first U.S. commanded military action fought on European soil. Hard fought it was, with the United States Army Air Service playing a significant role, as did the tanks under the direction of Colonel George S. Patton. While the American Expeditionary Forces lost more than 7,000 men, the battle was considered a success. Hyman Lashiwer was one of those casualties, and for his actions he was awarded the nation's second highest honor, the Distinguished Service Cross.

The formal Citation reads, "The President of the United States of America, authorized by Act of Congress, July 9, 1918, take pride in presenting the Distinguished Service Cross (Posthumously) to Private First

Class Hyman Lashiwer, United States Army, for extraordinary heroism in action while serving with Company M, 9th Infantry Regiment, 2nd Division, American Expeditionary Force, near Jaulny, France, September 12, 1918. Private Lashiwer, with three other soldiers, volunteered to carry wounded men of other companies from in front of our advanced positions and carried this work on under violent machine gun fire while a counterattack was developing." [7]

After lingering in a field hospital for three weeks, Hyman succumbed to his wounds. His uniformed body was buried in a cemetery just a little bit south of the small French village of Belleau, near a wood, where just a short time earlier, he had fought. His burial shroud was a burlap bag, his coffin an unadorned pine box. Not a Star of David, but a Christian Cross marked the plot in which his body was placed. Attached to it was a quarter-size, metal identification tag bearing his name, his unit and his rank. It is unlikely the reporting officer, Chaplain J. E. Doherty, recited Kaddish, the Jewish Prayer for the Dead. A simple gold ring inscribed with the initials E.N. and the date, 25-12-10, was interred with his remains, but the significance of the inscription is unknown. [8]

The small cemetery in which Hyman Lashiwer's was buried, is today's Aisne-Marne American Cemetery. The remains of 2,289 men who died in the war, are buried there.

After the armistice was signed, letters from the American Graves Registration Service were posted to Eva's College Point address, but her two replies came from St. Louis, Missouri. Sometime after the 1920 census, she had gone there to seek treatment for cancer. The first was her directive to ship Hyman's remains to New York City for burial. She also wrote the names of her brother Morris, living in Hartford, and her widowed mother Anna, living in the village of Nemirov, twenty miles north of Tulchin. In the second, she provided an address in Nemirov such that Anna Lashiwer might be told of her son's death, and asked her wishes. In closing, Eva signed this note with her maiden name, Lashiwer. [9] Not mentioned in any communication was Anna Lashiwer's husband, Philip. Presumably, he was no longer living.

Hyman's body was disinterred on January 19, 1922 and returned to America aboard the U.S. Army transport *Cantigny*. [10] On February 23rd, C. Johann & Sons brought his remains to College Point. Eva placed his coffin in a room arranged as a chapel, in the rear of a grocery store she had opened. Members of the Oscar Ammann Legion Post and the Ladies Auxiliary took part in a memorial service held in his honor, after which a firing squad from Fort Totten accompanied the cortege to Mount Hebron Cemetery in Flushing. There, Hyman's body was laid to rest with full military honors. [11] Named his War Risk Insurance beneficiary, Eva began receiving monthly checks from the United States Government, but they were soon to cease arriving.

According to a post-war newspaper article on his having been awarded the honor, Hyman Lashiwer did, at least for a short time, live in College Point with his sister. [12] He holds the sole distinction of being the only man with ties to the village, to be awarded the Distinguished Service Cross during World War One.

Ten months later, on the last day of December, Eva Kessler died from pancreatic cancer in St. Francis Hospital in Hartford. [13]She and Barnet had moved to Connecticut to be with her brother Morris, and his family. It was there she spent her final days. Eva is buried in Chesa Shel Emeth, a small Jewish cemetery in Hartford. Buried beside her are Morris who died in 1930, and Tillie, his wife, who died in 1959. [14] Barnet married twice more. He died in Far Rockaway, NY in November 1971. In the mid-1890's, Nemirov had a Jewish population numbering just under three thousand. Most of that population was lost in the Holocaust. [15]

32

Louis George Fritz

January 11, 1898 - October 6, 1918

L ouis George Fritz never knew his grandfather, after whom he was named. He had fought in, and survived wounds received, during the Civil War. He was one of the founding members of College Point's, Adam Wirth Grand Army of the Republic Post No. 451. Fritz had come to America from Germany before 1860, and lived all of his adult life working in Poppenhusen's factory. He was also saloon keeper. Ten children were born, one of them a son named Charles, arrived in 1869. [1] The veteran died in 1886, seven years before his grandson Louis George, came into the world. He was the second child of son Charles, and his wife, Mamie.

Not much is known of Louis' early life other than he was Catholic, and a 1912 graduate of P. S. 27. Three years later, he appeared in that year's census working as a plumber. As required, he registered for military service on September 9, 1918, not in College Point, but in Boston. This would be in the third, and ultimately final registration for the draft when men born between September 12, 1873, and September 12, 1900, were required to register. He listed the U.S. Shipping Board, and the *USS Meade* as his address. Two weeks earlier, Louis, and four other local men had joined the Merchant Marine. Doing so exempted them from military service. [2]

Built in Scotland in 1874, the *City of Berlin* was taken by the U.S. Government in 1898 and renamed the *Meade*. During the Spanish-American War, the vessel was used as a troop ship, and in January 1918, assigned to the Shipping Board. For the duration of the conflict, the *Meade* functioned as a training vessel in the preparation officers, engineers and sailors, to operate all the ships that moved troops and cargo, during, and ultimately after, the war. [3]

It was projected that more than 25,000 merchant sailors would be needed to man all the ships under construction. Most unusual for this service was that it involved the nation's 6,800 drug stores located in 6,300 cities, towns and villages in all the forty-eight states. For the nominal fee of one dollar a year, pharmacy owners and operators had agreed to set up a booth or counter in their places of business, and use it to make printed literature available describing the merchant shipping service. They were also sworn in as recruiting officers, and empowered to enroll recruits between the ages of 21 and 30. [4]

Usually the training course extended over a period of six weeks, and upon passing an examination in the particular course of training pursued, graduates were then placed on a merchant vessel for service. There were a variety of roles to be filled, sailor, cook, mess-man, fireman, oiler or water tender, among them. An additional incentive was the possibiliy for advancement. [5]

It was into this life that young Louis embarked in late August 1918, but his education aboard the *Meade* was short-lived. Almost four weeks to the day he arrived, Louis suffered a ruptured appendix, but an operation to resolve the matter, was not susccessful. [6] His parents were notified, and they immediately hastened to Boston. When they got there, they were unable to see him as the hospital ship was in quarantine, probably due to influenza. It was running rampant. Their son died on Sunday October 6th. Louis George Fritz was 21 years old. [7]

Undertaker C. Johann & Sons took charge, and returned his body to College Point. Louis' funeral was held in the home in which he'd been raised. St. Fidelis parish priest, Father George Bittermann, led the service after which an escort of eight sailors, mostly College Point men, his friends, accompanied the body to Flushing Cemetery. There he was given full military honors and laid to rest. [8]

33

Benjamin Franklin Blue

November 1881 - October 7, 1918

His father, after whom he was named, was famous for being the most noted sharpshooter the regular army had ever produced. For over thirty years he held the record for winning countless awards in numerous contests. [1] The source of the surname Blue is unknown, for he was enumerated in the 1850 and subsequent Pennsylvania census records, as being the first-born son of Samuel and Elizabeth Remsnyder. According to military service records, [2] and a pension application filed after his death, he enlisted in the Army in 1867 under that name. Each time his term of service came to an end, he rejoined.

He was sent to California in 1870, fought in the Modoc Indian War. With that experience behind, him he then battled gonorrhea and syphillis. Apparently, not all of his days out west were spent fighting Indians. When his third tour of duty began in 1875, he used the name, Benjamin F. Blue, for the first time. That happened at Willet's Point, Bayside, a post eventually named Fort Totten in honor of Civil War Brigadier General, Joseph G. Totten. [3]

Having garnered much recognition for his shooting skills, and risen to the rank of Sergeant, when his tour was up in 1880, he signed on again. He also married Louise Witzel and became father to three children. The first was named Benjamin Franklin Blue, Jr., born in Brooklyn in 1881. Two sisters followed, Louise and Minnie, both born on different army reservations, one in Colorado; the other in the Oklahoma Territory.

Sergeant Blue ended his military career at Fort Totten on December 31, 1897, his character rated excellent throughout his many postings. When the war with Spain came shortly thereafter, he offered to serve, but the army very graciously declined. He lived in Whitestone for a time then moved to College Point, where he lived until his death on March 10, 1912. [4] His remains were interred at Cypress Hills National Cemetery in Brooklyn. As a bugler sounded a mournful Taps, a firing squad fired a salute over his grave." [5] Blue's love of shooting was never far from his mind. In 1902 the *Brooklyn Daily Eagle* published his challenge "to meet all comers on the rifle range." [6] There is no record that anyone responded.

His wife applied for a pension based on her husband's thirty-year Army career. Numerous letters were written to the Pension Board with no positive reply. Responding to requests for documentation of his service, Louise remitted much of his memorabilia, his medals, and certificates, discharge papers etc. She then lamented their loss. [7] A final request to her Congressman brought about a response from the War Department. It was dated January 30, 1918 and explained that because Benjamin had not served during the Civil War, there was no way the Government would or could provide a pension. Less than a year later, Louise would receive a second letter from the War Department.

To say that Benjamin Franklin Blue Jr. was an army brat, would be to state the obvious. As was his father before him, young Benjamin was skilled with a rifle having qualified as a marksman and sharpshooter in 1899. [8] In the 1900 census he was enumerated as being neither in the army, nor did he even have a job. He was, in fact, a member of Company G in the 69th Regiment, the famed Irish Brigade of the Civil War. In competitive shooting this year, Corporal Blue qualified as expert; truly a chip off the old block. [9]

From his official burial record it is known that he was unmarried and a Bugler in Company D of the 10th Regiment of Engineers, a forestry unit. How he came to be in this unit is another mystery, but early in August 1917, the Forest Service, as part of the 10th Regiment of Engineers, advertised for recruits. Training took place on the campus of American University in Washington, DC. These men performed a very important service because for the first time in history, it was necessary to organize military forces specially trained and equipped to work in the forest. Wood was required for building roads and railroad beds, constructing barracks, erecting telephone poles, supporting trenches and every other wartime building and construction project. [10] The nation's foresters and lumbermen responded eagerly when the call came, but there is no indication Benjamin Blue had ever had anything to do with trees. The closest he came was working as a fireman on the Long Island Rail Railroad, feeding wood into steam locomotive furnaces. [11]

Apparently not everyone in a forestry unit was actively engaged in forestry work, and so it was with Benjamin Blue. He was, after all, a bugler. His job was to rouse the troops at reveille, announce mess, sick calls and numerous other attention-getting tattoos. Taps would be the end of every day. He enjoyed what he did so much that while confined to a bed in a base hospital, but saying he was getting better, he wrote a letter home that was published in the local newspaper. In it he quoted some of the humorous verbal jabs thrown his way, "Yes, that bugler sits around the guard tent all day while us Yahoos have to work." [12]

In spring and summer 1918, influenza outbreaks were reported in France. Early in July a flare-up occurred at Camp Valdahon where brigades of Field Artillery were regularly sent for special work. One would leave and another would arrive. A mild epidemic would run its course in a few weeks, and the disease would subside. Then another new brigade would enter the post, and within a few days, influenza would break out among these troops. This is how it usually went, thus it is probable the virus persisted in the barracks. [13]

Blue was billeted in one of these barracks at Camp Valdahon, and died in the Red Cross Hospital there on October 7th. The cause was attributed to bronchial pneumonia, but it was more likely influenza. His uniformed body was buried in Grave 132 in the U.S. Military Cemetery, and lay undisturbed until February 4, 1921. His remains were disinterred, placed in a new wooden coffin, and made ready for return to the United States. [14] On May 23rd, C. Johann and Sons brought them to College Point. Burial took place in the same Cypress Hills National Cemetery where his father had been interred with full military honors in 1912. The same honors were bestowed on Benjamin, Jr. in the presence of his mother and two sisters. [15]

Louise Blue died in College Point on June 8, 1942. She was eighty-two, buried with her husband, and probably unaware that her son was the first College Point soldier to die in France as a direct result of the epidemic that would claim the lives of millions of others, young and old, across the globe.

34

Louis Schmidt

August 23, 1897 - October 9, 1918

Five days after Louis Fritz was buried, it was reported that war relics, captured machine guns, rifle shells, field untensils, and other articles, were on display at the village's Bee Hive Café. It was also reported that a detachment of soldiers from Fort Totten had accorded military honors for another young College Point soldier, Louis Schmidt. [1] His time in the army, two weeks, was even shorter than Louis George Fritz's in the Merchant Marine. With an eight month age difference, and both having graduated from P.S. 27, there is no doubt they would have known each other.

With high school attendance not in his cards, Louis Schmidt had registered for the draft fifteeen months earlier saying he was employed by the Rainier Motor Car Company in Flushing. Inducted on September 26th, young Schmidt was not long in training at Camp Upton, when on October 9th, he died from pneumonia brought on by an attack of influenza. [2]

It is quite likely Louis Schmidt never held a rifle, much less fired one. Like many others at Camp Upton, when he fell ill, Private Schmidt reported to the camp hospital seeking something to make him feel better. There were no miracle drugs in 1918 to combat an illness about which next to nothing was known. Treatment was limited to tender loving care administered by the nurses on staff.

In the days preceding his induction, the first deaths from Influenza, also called Spanish Flu, were reported at Upton, and other training camps around the country. Eight thousand men had come down with the respiratory illness at Fort Devens in Massachusetts. At the same time, similar infections prompted the Commander of Fort Lee in Petersburg, Virginia to prohibit religious services. The submarine base in Groton, Connecticut was placed under quarantine. [3] Before long, Camp Upton was closed indefinitely, with 170 suffering young men in the base hospital. In the midst of war news, censorship, and no requirement on the part of physicians to report deaths from pneumonia, or even flu, the outbreak was pretty much underreported or not at all. [4] Charles Mahler's death in March had been attributed to pneumonia, very likely one of those taken as a matter of course.

According to New York City Health Commissioner Royal S. Copeland, "There is no danger of the infection spreading here," [5] but within days he announced that more cases had been discovered. He also said there was no cause for alarm. [6] This was followed by a *New York Times* article originating in Washington speculating that influenza had been brought to America via German U-boats. "It is quite possible the epidemic was started by Huns sent ashore by Boche submarine boats, for they have been in New York and other places. The Germans have started epidemics in Europe; there is no reason why they should be particularly gentle with America." [7]

Fear was beginning to surface that the disease having found entry to New York, was likely to spread, and spread rapidly. All schools, churches, synagogues, and theaters closed. Baseball games were banned, and racing cards were cancelled. Saloons shut their doors; department stores curtailed their business hours. In an attempt at calming the public, the Surgeon General issued twelve guidelines on how to avoid respiratory diseases. He recommended that people breathe through their noses, chew their food well, drink two glasses of water upon waking up in the morning, and avoid wearing tight clothes, tight shoes, and tight gloves. He also suggested staying away from crowds and covering mouths when coughing or sneezing. [8]

In the weeks to come, the number of reported cases ebbed and flowed, one day raging, another day coming under control. In early October, Copeland announced that his department had found, and would soon put a vaccine into general use that would prevail over the "Spanish Influenza." Meanwhile, no one could explain why so many soldiers and sailors, young men of full vitality with the best of habits, living much out of doors, seemed to yield so easily to this disease." [9]

In College Point, influenza claimed the life of Carrie Mottram, thirty-two year-old wife of Rev. Benjamin Mottram, pastor of St. Paul's Episcopal Church. [10] The disease also claimed another local man, Joseph Schmidt, a thrity-eight year-old watchman at the College Point Boat Company. [11] While his surname was the same, he was not related to Louis.

As October drew to a close, it appeared the disease was losing its grip. Significant reductions in the number of cases were eported, not only in New York City, [12] but also at military installations. [13] Ten thousand soldiers at Camp Dix, New Jersey had voluntarily taken the vaccine treatment, and not one had contracted pneumonia. The treatment was considered a success. [14] In hindsight, it can be said that the epidemic had peaked, and was beginning to wane. The public was warned to remember that there was as yet no specific cure for influenza. While many alleged cures and remedies were being recommended, they often did more harm than good." [15] The country was not yet out of the woods, and business was still badly hampered. People were being told to stay off the streets, unless they had important business to transact. [16]

By mid-November, newspapers were calling the epidemic "A Thing of the Past," but with cold season coming on, every cough and sneeze was a cause for alarm. Not to worry, "Get a small bottle of Elly's Cream Balm from your druggist, and apply a little of this fragrant antiseptic cream in your nostrils." [17] If Elly's Cream didn't do the trick, then a healthy application of Vick's VapoRub on the head, throat and back, was a good way to, "stimulate the air passages." [18] It was advertised as a "preventative", and for the moment, it appeared the epidemic had run its course. But there would be a curtain call.

It is estimated that 675,000 died in America, ten times as many who died in battle. [19] Spread worldwide through 1918 - 1919, Influenza moved easily through military populations, the result of many men living in close quarters. In six months, the disease killed some thirty million people around the globe. This number was more than three times the number of military casualties suffered by all of the belligerents during more than four years of fighting in World War One. [20]

Private Louis Schmidt's funeral took place on October 13th. Burial was in Flushing Cemetery, Rev. Arthur Halfmann of St. John's Lutheran Church, conducting the service. [21] A detachment of soldiers from Fort Totten was present and accorded military honors to the young soldier. [22] Though he had neither died in battle, nor aboard a ship at sea, at the time of his death Louis was in the service of his country. His parents, both German immigrants, and his seven siblings, all sisters, mourned his loss.

35

August William Breisacher

June 15, 1888 - October 12, 1918

Above the newspaper report of August William Breisacher's funeral was the headline, "To Honor Fallen Heroes". [1] Not mentioned in this short entry was Louis Doerr. His remains, and August's had been transported back to American soil aboard the same U.S. Army transport *Wheaton*, likely prompting the editor to use the plural form of hero. Before their life in the army, both had worked at the American Hard Rubber Company, and so they might have known each other. Doerr was younger by four years, raised in the Lutheran Church, and noted for his athletic prowess. Breisacher was Catholic, the eldest of five children, two brothers, Fred and William, and two sisters, Anna and Margaret. Until his death was announced in 1918, the name August Breisacher had not appeared in any newspaper.

On June 5, 1917, ten days shy of his 30th birthday, August registered for the draft. He described himself as being tall yet stout, with dark brown hair. At the time, he was working for John H. Gerlach, who had made his fortune manufacturing and binding loose-leaf books. His factory gave jobs to many College Point people. Fred also did his duty. He labored at the American Hard Rubber Company. Both registrants were unmarried, and both claimed sole responsibility for their parents' welfare. [2]

At some point during the following eleven months, August joined Fred at the rubber company. The army came calling for August at the start of May. Within three days of induction, he was transferred three times, his final assignment, Company E, 114th Infantry. [3] His first two weeks of Army life were spent at Fort Slocum on the New York City/Westchester County border.

In the ideal world, he was supposed to receive six weeks of initial training, but his preparation for war did not last anywhere near that long. Shortly after arrival, he was sent to Camp McClellan in Anniston, Georgia. Once again he was there for but a brief time, departing for Europe in mid-June aboard the U.S. Army transport *Covington*. [4] As had happened to others, there were no brass bands to cheer them on, no family, no sweethearts, wives or friends to wave goodbye. There hadn't even been time enough for August's family to see him just one time in his army uniform. They did, however, get to see Fred in his, owing to his July 23rd induction into a unit that did not go overseas, Company K, 68th Infantry.

Following arrival, the 114th crossed France to the trenches between the Vosges Mountains and the Alps on the Swiss border. Training began with special attention given to gas tactics. Had August been inducted a year earlier, a portion of his training would have explained how to deal with it. New soldier that he was, this preparation was very likely his very first exposure to chemical warfare. [5]

In mid-September, the regiment had it first experience when the Germans commenced a heavy artillery barrage that included shells containing the mustard version. They rained down incessantly. Sentries failed to give warning. The men put on, took off and changed their gas masks in confusion resulting in panic. Company officers on the scene proved ignorant of what to do. [6] Private August Breisacher became one of 256 gas victims. [7] Another, was College Point man Walter E. J. Garvin, serving in Company E. They had been inducted on the same day in May; he was wounded slightly. [8]

It cannot be said for certain, but it is possible that due to his lack of adequate training, Breisacher might have taken off his mask too quickly following the attack. It is also possible that his mask might have been stripped off due to the concussion of the exploding artillery shells. However it happened, he survived the artillery attack and the gassing, thus enabling him to take part in one more engagement.

On the morning of October 12th, the 114th began an attack against a heavily defended wooded area called Bois D'Ormont near Verdun. These were strongly fortified heights, and they had to be taken before the attack could be continued. The Germans had built a line of concrete machine gun pillbox positions along the edge of the woods. The machine gunners simply went into their concrete dugouts, then came out and aimed their guns. The 114th, advancing from the south, penetrated to the center of the Bois d'Ormont, but not without heavy losses. One of its attacking companies went into action with 192 men, and within two hours had suffered more than 100 casualties. [9] August Breisacher was once again numbered among them; killed in action. [10] According to all the military authorities, it was one of the worst slaughters of the entire war,. [11]

Other College Pointers in the 114th taking part in the battle included Charles Globe, Company A, and Henry Hoffmann, also in Breisacher's Company E. Globe came through unscathed, but Hoffman was wounded slightly, perhaps gassed, since the terms were frequently used interchangeably. [12] Walter Garvin, wounded with August Breisacher on September 16th, sustained another more serious would during this battle. He was also captured and spent the rest of his time in France in a German prisoner of war camp. In a letter sent home he wrote, "I was wounded and lay in No Man's Land for three days before being captured by the Huns." [13]

On the day he died, August's uniformed body, the uniform his family never got to see him wearing, was placed in a pine box, and buried in the Meuse-Argonne American Cemetery, Grave 38, Section 35, Plot 1. In late

November, the family was advised by telegram that their son and brother had been wounded in action. A second telegram arrived in mid-December stating that he had died from those wounds. His mother immediately dispatched a letter asking, "If he was only slightly wounded, I would like to know what they call slightly wounded when he died from those wounds?" She also requested the return of all of his personal belongings. for which there was no reply. [14]

In another letter dated February 4, 1919, his mother asked for a photograph of her son if one was available. Again, no response, thus there is no known photograph of August Breisacher in the uniform of his country. In mid-July, a local newspaper ran a story that said the bodies of the American soldiers killed in action would not be brought home from France. It prompted another letter reading, "We demand the beloved body of our son and brother be returned as soon as possible. He was born here in America and we want him buried in our family plot. We all think that it was hard enough that he was shipped over there without ever seeing him in his uniform, but now to think that we can never have his body is enough to drive us all insane. We are the ones that feel his loss, and not the French government." [15]

Released from his German prison, Walter Garvin arrived back in New York on March 12, 1919 aboard the U.S. Army transport *America*. [16] Globe and Hoffman finished their trans-Atlantic return to College Point via Newport News, VA, arriving on May 6, 1919, aboard the U.S. Army transport *Madawaska*. [17]

The coffin containing August Breisacher's remains arrived at Hoboken in early August, and brought to College Point. [18] On the last day of the month, the *Brooklyn Daily Eagle* ran the short piece with the headline, "To Honor Fallen Heroes" [19] When she received the telegram, the only thing his mother coud say was, "He went into the service on May 2nd and arrived overseas a month later." [20] Father George Bitterman celebrated his funeral Mass at St. Fidelis, and officiated at his burial. Together with members of the Oscar Ammann Post acting as pallbearers, a firing squad from Fort Totten escorted the procession to Flushing Cemetery. There, in the presence of his family, three volleys were fired and taps sounded, as the last tribute to this fallen hero. [21]

Margaret Breisacher died in August 1924. She was followed in death by her husband, two years later. Fred, who had never gone overseas, received his army discharge in February 1919, married, and was a house painter all his life. When he died in July 1973, he was buried at Long Island National Cemetery. His wife Mildred outlived him by nineteen years and is buried with him. Anna and Margaret Breisacher never married and never left College Point. William Breisacher married, moved to Flushing, and raised his family. He died at the age of thirty-seven in July 1940.

TO HONOR FALLEN HEROES

Private August W. Breisacher, 30 years old, son of Mr. and Mrs. August Breisacher of Schleicher's Court, College Point, who was killed in action at Bois de Ormont during the Meuse-Argonne offensive on Oct. 12, 1918, will be buried with full, military honors tomorrow afternoon in St. Michael's Cemetery, Flushing. Breisacher was a member of Co. E, 114th Infantry, 29th Division, when he fell in battle. He is survived by his parents, two brothers and two sisters. The funeral services will be in charge of the Oscar Ammann Post of the American Legion, of which Martin Zwicke is the commander.

36

John Baptist Endres

August 21, 1895 - October 18, 1918

By the day he was inducted into the Army, April 5, 1918, [1] twenty-two year-old John Baptist Endres, tall with blue eyes and blond hair, [2] had spent four years in a preparatory seminary in Indiana looking one day to being ordained a Catholic priest. [3] After graduating in 1916, he chose not to continue his studies and returned to his hometown. There he gained recognition as one of the village's stellar athletes, both on the diamond, and on the gridiron. Positioned alongside Lolly Doerr in 1915 and 1916, the duo played together on the College Point Athletic Association team. Closing out successful seasons both years, they took part in two memorable late-autumn games to decide which team would win the Greater New York City football championship. The College Point eleven won it all in 1915, with no opponent ever crossing the end zone. [4] A year later, Endres playing right guard next to Lolly at right tackle, they played the Elms of Manhattan to a 7-7 tie at Donnelly's Field. [5] Both games had attendance exceeding five thousand fans. Endres had also completed six months of service as one of New York's Finest attached to the 23rd Precinct in East Harlem. [6] He was also engaged to be married. His father, after whom he was named, had come to America from Germany in 1885. Around the turn of the century, his was one of several German bakeries in College Point. John Jr. had an older sister, Elizabeth, and a younger brother named William.

Arriving at Camp Upton, new recruit Endres was initially assigned to the 152nd Depot Brigade, and was then sent to Camp Wadsworth, in Spartanburg, South Carolina. Shortly thereafter, he was transferred to the newly formed 106th Machine Gun Battalion. [7] With a more mechanized war in the offing, it had quickly become clear that the nation had a greater need for machine gunners than it did for horse-riding cavalry units. To soothe the feelings of these fighting men, the army's leaders told them, "machine gunners had to be the brainiest men in the service." [8] Endres had the qualifications, but no one was fooled. Before long, the 106th was Europe-bound, and the inevitable eastward journey by rail across France.

In early August, the unit pitched tents in the villlage of Oudezeele, where John had the chance to see fellow College Pointer William Pauly cavort in a theatrical extravaganza put on by the players of the 27th Division. As per usual, Pauly was dressed in drag.

Privates Jack Roche and William C. Pauly in
their dance specialty "Whisper of the Moon"

Following this welcome diversion, the 106th continued its eastward
sojourn, and on September 2nd, John penned one of his many letters to his
parents and family. Written from "Somewhere in France", it read, "It is
over two weeks now since I have heard from you last and I am beginning
to feel uneasy about it. It makes me think that something is wrong at home.
I was waiting for a letter from you before I wrote, but it is taking too long.
I am getting along fine and hope everything at home is the same. You told
me in your last letter about George Barrett being wounded and the next
day I see his name in the Paris edition of the New York Herald. I met
William Thorogood over here one day and he told me about Ed Martin
being missing since June 24. I suppose this will not be news to you, because
you most likely knew it before I did. I think winter is setting in over here
already, because it is mighty cold in the evening. This writing paper is from
the Red Cross."

John had always played an integral part in working with the people his parents hired to work in the bakery. In this letter, his concerns appear to be about the bakery and its operation. [9]

On the 19th of September, the football teams of the 1st and 3rd platoons met in battle on a makeshift football field. Endres, playing for the former, was on the starting team. His performance was noteworthy, even though the game wound up in a tie. Three days later, Company "C" met and defeated Company "B". Endres again proved to be the individual star. [10]

On the evening of September 26th, the company arrived at the real western front, and prepared for its role in the battle of the Hindenburg Line. After eight days of terrible fighting, the Allies succeeded in breaking through the famous line. Endres came through unscathed. For the next three weeks, 106th took to the roads in search of an enemy in retreat, witnessing the effects of the hard fighting that had taken place. Unburied dead lay in hundreds, destroyed field pieces and captured ones lined the way; shattered machine gun nests were innumerable. [11]

During the cold, cold evening of October 16th, in the light of a full moon, the company moved into a little field on the outskirts of the town of Escanfort near St. Souplet. The battle-fatigued soldiers spent the night carrying equipment to the position and digging trenches and emplacements for the guns for the barrage in support of the advancing 107th Infantry that was to commence at 5:40 the next morning, and promptly it did. After some delay, the 107th came up and Endres' machine gun company comprised of four guns at this point, cautiously made its way toward Jonc de Mer Farm. It was an awful sight of debris, dead animals, dead Germans, dirt and neglect everywhere and there passed another night, this one under a heavy rain that did not let up until nine o'clock the next morning. When dawn broke cold and damp, the din of the Allies' artillery barrage as well as that emanating from the German artillery greeted Endres' waking hours. There were also three to four inches of water in his shell hole billet. [12]

At 5:30 A.M. on October 18th, for the first and last time in his entire army career, John Baptist Endres moved forward with the attack. Heretofore, the 106th had been limited to support by barrage only. His unit advanced across the field in front of Jonc de Mer Farm, and in that place encountered a German machine gun nest. The bullets tore into him fracturing the left side of his skull, and his right leg below the knee at the same time blowing off his right foot. [13] He had fought at Dickebusche in Belgium, survived the Battle of the Hindenburg Line and met his death courageously at St. Souplet. [14]

Clothed in his uniform and overcoat, the deceased Pvt. John B. Endres was buried with all honors possible in Grave 22 in the Military Cemetery at St. Souplet, which later became the Somme American Cemetery. [15] Two months later on New Year's Eve, John B. Endres Sr. sold his bakery. [16]

His son's body was disinterred on February 3, 1921, and prepared for return to the United States. Because he had been a member of the New York City Police Department prior to the war, his casket was received, placed upon a caisson by the Police Department and escorted to Cypress Hills Cemetery in Brooklyn. [17] There in the presence of his family, two police lieutenants, four sergeants, 65 policemen and a firing squad composed of eight patrolmen, a sergeant and two buglers, John Baptist Endres, Jr. was buried with full honors, police and military, on April 12, 1921 in Section 18, Police Honor Legion Grave 34. [18]

On June 20, 1923, a parade through lower Manhattan paid tribute to the war service of 827 members of the city's police force, eighteen of which died for their country. A memorial tablet containing the names of those casualties was placed at the head of the staircase in police headquarters. When the official program was concluded, the former service men of the department marched up the steps and saluted before the tablet. [19] It is not known if John's parents and family attended, but it is very likely they did. In 1973, the city opened a new headquarters, and this building fell into limbo until 1988, when it was converted into cooperative apartments. The whereabouts of the memorial tablet is unknown.

John's sister Elizabeth had married John Schmermund in 1915, and continued to live in College Point until her death in 1959. His brother William married late in life, and for reasons unknown committed suicide in the summer of 1960. John Endres, Sr. died by his own hand as well in May 1940. His wife Elizabeth died nineteen months later, in December 1941.

William Thorogood, referred to by John Endres in his letter from France, served in the Headquarters Company of the 105th Infantry. Born in Scotland, he came to America in 1905 when he was five years old. Coincidentally, on the day John B. Endres died, Thorogood was severely wounded, but recovered from his wounds, and was able to return home. [20]

37

Thomas Joseph McCormick

December 24, 1896 – October 23, 1918

Fudging on the truth, Thomas J. McCormick claimed he had reached the required age of twenty-one, when on June 5, 1917, he arrived at Cleveland, Ohio Draft Board # 6 to register. What brought him to the shores of Lake Erie is unknown, but covering all his bases he wrote he was born in Clinton, Massachusetts, and provided three mailing addresses. One was in College Point, a second in Manhattan, and a third, where he was currently living in Cleveland. He did not say the College Point address was that of his mother, Annie Fay McCormick. He wrote also that he was unemployed, unmarried, worked as a machinist, and had been previously rejected for military service due to eye issues. At the end of the day, because of those visual problems, he was rejected a second time. [1] In the only photo known to exist, his left eye looks a little lazy possibly caused by a condition known as strabismus, [2] a vision condition in which a person is unable to align both eyes simultaneously under normal conditions, which can affect depth perception. His draft card plainly states, "Rejected, eye sight."

Eye problems not withstanding, eleven months later he was called up for service and assigned to the 152nd Depot Brigade at Camp Upton. Within a short time, he was transferred to another unit, Battery C, 303rd Field Artillery. [3] In a touch of irony, life had taken him full circle in that his new unit trained at Camp Devens in Ayer, Massachusetts, twenty miles north of the Worcester County town where he was born. [4]

Thomas was one of a group of about one hundred men who arrived at Devens from Camp Upton on May 26th, and departed very early on the morning of July 16th, bound for Europe aboard the U.S. Army transport *Miltiades.* Following arrival at Newport in Wales on July 31st, the 303rd was broken up. Training cadres were formed and prepared for their role as replacements for combat divisions at the front. [5]

Near to Clermont-Ferrand, almost in the heart of France, stood the villages of Aubiere and Ceyrat. It was here that Thomas and his mates began intensive training on the use of an artillery piece called the 155 G.P.F. The letters stood for Grande Portée Filloux. A French Army Lieutenant, surname Filloux, had invented a long-range gun, nineteen feet five inches long, weighing 8,520 pounds. The hugh artillery piece was capable of shooting a projectile with a range of about ten miles. The French Military named the weapon in his honor, the English translation being, "Long Range Filloux. " In a war in which the relatively small 75-mm gun was the standard artillery weapon of the Allies, this was a big gun. [6]

While Thomas was being schooled in the fine points of heavy artillery his brother John was stationed with the 26th Infantry regiment, 240 miles slightly northeast of Clermont-Ferrand, very near to the front. Though born in 1899, he had managed to enlist in the regular army in December 1916. [7] Within six months, the unit was in France part of the initial group of 1st Division soldiers that played roles in numerous battles winning many citations and awards, but at a terrible cost. Over nine hundred members of the 26th Regiment lost their lives in a six-month period. By war's end, the unit had fought in places with names familiar at the time,

Montdidier-Noyon; Aisne-Marne; St Mihiel; Meuse-Argonne; Lorraine and Picardy. [8]

The Meuse-Argonne Offensive had begun in the early morning of September 26th with a gargantuan artillery barrage. Over the course of the next few days, the flu was as much in evidence, as were the exploding shells. On the 29th, General Pershing ordered a halt to the offensive due to a combination of factors; heavy rain, German reserves strengthening their defensive lines and increasing number of troops hit by that flu. As a result, on the 30th, the Americans found it necessary to call retreat, the first time this had happened in the course of the war. [9] On this day, the attack in the Argonne Forest broke down into pockets of small unit actions, and sometime during the night, one of those exploding artillery shells severely wounded John McCormick in both legs. He lay unattended for hours, all the time in massive pain, and it was not until morning that he was finally picked up. Gangrene had set in, and one leg had to be amputated above the knee. While most of the calf of his other leg was also seriously damaged, John insisted it be saved. [10]

The telegram telling of her son's massive injuries was delivered to Annie's Bronx apartment to which she had moved after both sons had entered the service. [11] If he did not already know it, she undoubtedly passed the news on to Thomas, not long into his training at Clermont-Ferrand. As the end of October drew near, Thomas became ill and was transported to Base Hospital 30, two miles from his training camp in the village of Royat. All hopes were for a speedy recovery. The hospital was well staffed treating hundreds of wounds and gas injuries, and witnessed the beginning of the influenza pandemic among the troops. [12] At 8:30 in the morning of October 23rd, influenza claimed the life of Thomas Joseph McCormick, [13]

"The flu took off another of our men today. McCormick died at Royat after several days of game fighting for his life. He was a well-liked lad and will make the fourth Battery C man we have buried." [14] For the second time in a matter of weeks, a telegram was delivered to Annie Fay McCormick.

There was an American Cemetery near Clermont-Ferrrand, and it was here two days following his death, that Thomas's uniformed body was laid to rest in Grave No. 10. [15] The sleeve of his tunic held the unit's emblem, an artillery shell of black fabric on which had been stitched in gold thread, the numbers 303, the shell form sewn on a circle of red cloth, perhaps 2" or 3" in diameter. He wore it proudly, if not for long, one would imagine.

Spring 1919, occasioned a letter from the Graves Registration Service asking Annie where she would wish her son to be buried? In her initial reply, she requested her son's body be returned to America. [16] It was followed up by a second asking that he be "laid to rest in Cypress Hills National Cemetery in Brooklyn. "It will be near to me and I can feel that I can visit. Give my boy all the honor as he deserves." In this letter, she also offered some information on her son's life, saying he had returned to her at age fourteen. Annie had spent most of her life working as a servant, been widowed twice, buried one child, and had another who was institutionalized. Because of her limited financial circumstance, both Thomas and John had probably been placed in an orphanage or institution, but "when the call came for him to serve his country, she wrote, Thomas went gallantly, and thought of his mother." "His brother is also a world war veteran," she continued, "totally disabled, but I have one consolation, I am not alone in my great sorrow. There are thousands of others." [17]

The body of Thomas J. McCormick was disinterred on March 8, 1921, and returned to the United States aboard the U.S. Army transport *Wheaton*. [18] Following arrival at Hoboken, NJ on June 7th, C. Johann and Sons removed the casket bearing his remains directly to Cypress Hills National Cemetery. [19] There he was buried as his mother had requested, in Section 2, Grave 8391. Cypress Hills being a National Cemetery, military honors were undoubtedly accorded.

John McCormick was released from Walter Reed Army Hospital on August 3, 1920, his Surgeon's Certificate of Disability set at 100%. For a short time, he studied music at the Julliard, and in 1923, married Bridget Mannion. A son was born a year later, and named Thomas in memory of the uncle he would never know. Another son followed, and was named after his father. The music career did not pay enough to support a family, but coincidentally, John had the good fortune to benefit from a friendship with

Theodore Roosevelt's son Archibald, under whom he had served. "Archie" was instrumental in getting him a civil service job at the Post Office, and for a time, John was able to walk aided by a prosthetic leg. So severe was the wound that amputation was eventually required. John McCormick died in March 1957. Bridget outlived him by thirty-five years, passing away in July 1990. [20] Both are buried in Long Island National Cemetery.

Annie Faye McCormick died at Queens General Hospital in January 1948, and was buried in Saint Mary's Cemetery in Flushing. According to her great grandson John McCormick, her life had been filled with much sadness, yet she was the sweetest lady in the world, and showed not a tinge of resentment for the shabby way life had treated her. She's one person I would have liked to have known." [21] Exactly how long she lived in College Point is unclear, but it is known that Thomas lived with her for at least a short time before induction, in a three-story, wood frame apartment style building next door to the Poppenhusen Institute. [22] Both Thomas and John McCormick are remembered as sons of College Point.

38

Albert W. Frey

February 22, 1889 - November 4, 1918

A lbert Frey almost did not live past his seventh birthday. In November 1896, young Albert, a friend, Otto Muhlenbrink, and a third boy, John Kraebel, were seriously injured by an explosion of gunpowder. It had been set aside for use in the village's parade to celebrate the election of William McKinley as President. The local Republican club had its headquarters in the Turn Hall, a gymnasium and meeting place established after the Civil War. It was operated by Muhlenbrink's father. It was also the storing place for the powder to be used in the community's evening festivities. Aware of its presence, Muhlenbrink, the younger, along with his companions, decided to use it for their own jollification. After Otto lit the match igniting the powder, an explosion followed. It burned all three boys about the face and hands, Otto most seriously. [1] Fortuitously, the trio survived. Of the three, only Frey went to war.

Albert's father, Edward, owned a local printing company that published a weekly German language newspaper called the *Long Island Free Press*. In 1900, he and his wife Anna were parents to four children. Edward was the oldest followed by Albert, Minnie and Freda. By 1910, another daughter named Elsie had joined the family. Albert, now twenty-one, was working alongside his father, active in the life of the community, and at the Poppenhusen Institute, where he was a talented student in the woodworking class. [2]

When he registered for the draft, he wrote that he was unmarried, of medium height and build, with blue eyes and brown hair, working as a printer. Six days later, his father died after a lingering illness. [3] In the previous January, he had transferred management of the family business over to Albert. [4]

On October 10th, twenty-five men from College Point, Albert among them, were given a glorious send-off to Camp Upton. The soon-to-depart recruits were paraded through the streets of the town. Escorted by the Boy Scouts led by two fife, bugle and drum corps to Public School No. 27, it was only a few short months ago that most, if not all, had been poked, prodded and otherwise importuned. With Rev. Benjamin Mottram, rector of St. Paul's presiding, Father Schumack imparted a blessing upon all of them. At the end of the meeting, the College Point chapter of the Red Cross presented comfort kits to the embarking embryo soldiers. [5] Five days later, owing to her husband's death and the drafting of her son, Anna Frey advertised the sale of the printing plant. [6]

Reporting as ordered to the 152nd Depot Brigade, the so-called largest brigade in the Uncle Sam's Army, Albert began experiencing all the joys of being a soldier. In late November, he was sent to Camp Gordon, assigned to the 11th Company, 3rd Training Battalion, [7] and made top sergeant of his company in the quartermaster's department. [8] His engagment to a College Point girl, Frederica Schneeman, was announced in March, [9] and by mid-April he'd sailed for England, then on to France a member of Company A, 327th Infantry. [10] Sadly, no letters to Frederica survive, even though they would offer very little additional information. Cesnorship imposed strict limitations as to what could and could not be written.

At the end of summer, the 327th took part in the St. Mihiel Offensive, September 12-15. During this time, 129 men were wounded, 36 were lost, 25 killed in action and 11 died from wounds received. It was then held in reserve until, on the 24th, the soldiers moved south to the vicinity of Triaucourt and Rarecourt on the eastern edge of the Argonne Forest. The Meuse-Argonne Offensive began two days later, but the 327th did not join the fight until the end of the first week in October. From the 6th on, Frey and his Company A mates saw a great deal of action battling the German army defending the *Kriemhilde Stellung*, a "dense network of prepared killing grounds the Germans had created between the Meuse River and the Argonne Forest. Situated at the eastern end of the Hindenburg Line, it was the last and deadliest of the major German defensive positions." While advances were made, massive German counter-attacks forced retreats; the Hindenburg Line could not be lost. [11]

When dawn broke on October 11th, the 327th Infantry had been in continuous heavy fighting for four days and nights. They had had neither hot food nor coffee, nevertheless they were in position for yet another attack. The objective was a heavily fortified ridge above a road between the villages of Sommerance and St. Juvin. Just before five in the morning, instructions were received to postpone the attack. But as it happened, advance troops had gone forward without benefit of anticipated tank, and artillery support. In spite of heavy mist, intense machine gun fire and artillery barrage, they made good progress, but strong resistance forced a withdrawal. Back and forth went the battle throughout the morning, until late in the afternoon as the enemy slowly and reluctantly retreated, the 327th reached its objective. The ridge was taken, but not without heavy losses. [12] One among them was Albert Frey, the victim of a German machine gun sniper. In a letter written to his mother from Base Hospital No. 22, he told her he'd lain in a shell hole for a day and a half before being rescued, and that he suffered terriby with six bullets lodged in his right arm, hip and back. Recovery, he added, would take at least six weeks. [13]

Receiving the best care possible, he lingered for three weeks in the hospital near Bordeaux on the southwestern coast of France. But on November 4th, one week before the armistice ending hostilities would be signed, Albert Frey died of septicemia. [14] Had he lived, the nature of his wounds surely would have left him paralyzed from the waist down.

Two days later, with requisite military honors, his uniformed body was buried in A.E.F. Cemetery Number 27, his grave, number 108, marked by a cross. [15] The army notified his mother, and she in turn passed along the sad news to Edward, Frieda, Elsie and Minnie. Frederica Schneeman was also told. He would be the last College Point man to die in World War One as a result of wounds received in battle, but he would not be the last College Point man to die wearing the uniform of his country.

In mid-October 1920, Albert's remains were returned to College Point aboard the U.S. Army transport *Pocahontas*, [16] and buried in Flushing Cemetery with full military honors. [17] At the end of summer 1921, Anna Frey sold the family home and moved to Westchester County to live with her son Edward and his family. [18]

Five years later, in November, the War Department processed and approved her application to have a marker placed at her son's grave. Due to the large number of similar requests from all over the country, the marker was not shipped until April, two years later.[19] Anna lived on until her death in Chappaqua, New York in March 1935. [20] She was seventy-six, and still living with her son, and his family

Edward Frey, Jr. had sustained a serious injury to his right hand in 1901, [21] rendering him ineligible for military service. He married in 1910, became a public school teacher, but did not abandon the world of printing. He spent a thirty-five year career in education, during which he developed "The Print Ed Program". It became the graphic arts curriculum for the New York City Board of Education, and was used widely in secondary schools and community colleges for over sixty years. He also worked in collaboration with Columbia University, and was very involved in the Adult Education Program at the Poppenhusen Institute. Edward Frey had a life-long love of fine typography, accumulating a huge archive of catalogs, paper samples, and scrapbooks, replete with print-related ephemera.

Following on Edward's death in 1981, his family donated his massive collection to the Museum of Printing in North Andover, Massachusetts. [22]

39

William John Nicholas Mohrmann

May 19, 1894 - November 9, 1918

The armistice ending the war was signed in a French railway car at 11:00 o'clock in the morning on the 11th day of the 11th month of 1918. Two days earlier, Machinists Mate 2nd Class William John Nicholas Mohrmann died in his bed in the hospital on the water facing Long Island Sound at the Pelham Bay Naval Training Station. The official cause of his death was suppurative pleurisy preceded by influenza contracted just three weeks earlier. [1] William's parents, William and Dorothy, were German immigrants. His father sold groceries from his little store a few doors away from the Poppenhuseun Institute; a sister, Wilhelmina, had been born in 1902. The family moved to College Point prior to 1910, and traveled back and forth to Germany multiple times. By 1917, and out of school, William went to work for Kirkman and Sons, a Brooklyn firm selling soap products. After registering for the draft, [2] he continued working until May 1918, when he enlisted in the U. S. Navy Reserve Force. Shortly thereafter, he was sent to Pelham Bay. [3]

Of the more than one hundred College Point men whose service in the U.S. Navy can be documented, more than a third of them did some or all of their basic training at the Pelham Bay Naval Reserve Training Station. There were three major areas on the base, the first being what was called the probation camp. It was here that new recruits spent the first twenty-one days being vaccinated, inoculated and taught the fundamentals of navy life. The second area was a large parade ground flanked on two sides by housing, seventy-eight barracks, and the various administration buildings. Located near the shore and away from the center of activity stood the hospital, one of the largest and best of its kind. [4]

While his time in the Navy was not long, less than six months, Mohrmann was undoubtedly familiar with these three areas. One of the buildings housed a library where, if he took out a book, he would have seen the possibly familiar face of Miss Blanche Galloway. She was the only woman among 10,000 men on the post. She was also the former head librarian in College Point's Library. It had been the first of the Carnegie libraries built in 1904, when Pittsburgh steel magnate and philanthropist Andrew Carnegie donated $5.2 million dollars to establish a branch library system in New York City. College Point was selected to be the premier site. [5]

The navy had wanted a man for the job, in the mistaken belief that a woman's presence would upset the camp. Officials consented to hiring Galloway on a temporary basis only after some persuasion, and because no man was available. It did not take very long for the brass to acknowledge how exceptional Galloway was, and in a very short time, the objections to having a woman on duty at the camp, vanished. In a very unusual accommodation, a special housing unit was built that made it possible for her to reside at the training center. [6]

The onset of influenza at Naval facilities across the country began in Boston in late August 1918. Three cases were reported. There were eight more cases the next day, and fifty the day after that. Onset was very sudden. Patients frequently passed within an hour or two from an apparent healthy condition into a state of prostration. Outbreaks followed promptly in practically all nearby naval stations. At Newport, the epidemic began on September 10th, reached its peak seven days later, then terminated. In the last week of September, fifty cases appeared at the submarine base in New London. [7]

During this time, New York City area naval stations seemed to have escaped the epidemic, but late in September, Pelham Bay reported its first cases. By early October, fourteen sailors had died. The epidemic lasted through the end of the month, and by the first week of November, it appeared deaths from the illness at the station, had all but disappeared. When William Mohrmann died on November 9th, his death was one of only two reported. Compared to other naval facilities, Pelham Bay had very high influenza and mortality rates. There would be only one more death in November, and eighteen throughout the entire month of December. [8]

The 1918 - 1919 influenza pandemic killed more people than any other outbreak of disease in human history. Most 1918 influenza-related deaths were due to bacterial pneumonia. The lowest estimate of the death toll is twenty-one million, while recent scholarship estimates from fifty to one hundred million dead. World population was then only 28% of what is today, and most deaths occurred in a sixteen-week period, from mid-September to mid-December of 1918. [9]

Prior to William's burial, the College Point Chapter of the International Order of Odd Fellows, the Masons of which he was a member, held ritualistic services at the home of his parents. At two o'clock in the afternoon on November 13th, Rev. Arthur Halfmann, pastor of St. John's, laid his body to rest in Flushing Cemetery. [10] Perhaps because it was but two days following the signing of the armistice, there was no newspaper coverage mentioning graveside military honors, or a bugler playing taps. It can only be hoped that honors were accorded.

William Mohrmann, Sr. died during Memorial Day services in 1940. His now married daughter, Wilhelmina, had tried to discourage her father from marching in the College Point parade. His health was delicate, but he was reluctant to quit. "I'm the marshall's aide," he told her "a few pains and aches can't stop me." He collapsed and died as he prepared to step off in the line of march. [11] Dora Mohrmann lived on until December 1953. A Gold Star Mother, and long standing member of the Oscar Ammann Auxiliary, it was she who was memorialized after her passing. [12]

40

Henry Zimmer

February 23, 1888 - May 6, 1919

Henry Zimmer fought in and survived battles waged at the St. Mihiel Salient and in the Argonne Forest, and he did, in fact, make it back to America alive. It is heartbreaking to think that for all his time in France, Henry managed to escape all the enemy bullets and shells, and then die of meningitis. From day one his life had been a challenge. By the time he had barely passed his twelfth birthday, his uncle had killed himself by drinking poison, [1] his father had deserted the family, and his mother had died of stomach cancer. [2]

Clara Decker and Peter Zimmer married in the early 1880. They had three children, Clara Christine, and Henry, followed by William, born in 1892. Peter abandoned his family in 1891. Clara was then diagnosed with the cancer that took her life in 1900, [3] whereupon the three orphaned and abandoned Zimmer children went to live with their paternal grandmother.

According to the 1910 census, twenty-two year-old Henry worked at one of College Point's silk factories, and in mid-winter this same year, his father paid a short visit to College Point. He was "pleased to be hailed by former townsmen in various places." [4] There is nothing to indicate he sought out his former in-laws, or his children.

Unmarried, and employed at the Sunset Silk Mill in Brooklyn, Henry registered for the draft, and was called up in early April 1918. Assigned first to the 152nd Depot Brigade at Camp Upton, he was subsequently sent to Camp Wadsworth in Spartanburg to complete his training.[5] As a member of the 53rd Pioneer Infantry formed out of the 47th Infantry of the Brooklyn National Guard, he sailed from Hoboken in August 1918, aboard the *USS Mongolia*. [6] Arriving in France, the Pioneers were engaged chiefly in bridge building along with transporting ammunition and supplies. The unit also got involved in the fighting, becoming part of the great St. Mihiel offensive, and subsequent battles fought by the American Army.

Following the Armistice, the 53rd was stationed at various French towns and outposts eventually disembarking from Brest to America on April 22, 1919. Henry began the crossing as a patient in the ship's hospital and was alive when the vessel docked in Newport News, Virginia on May 4th. [7] The doctor who signed the Commonweatlth of Virginia Death Certificate stated he attended Henry until his death two days later, citing the the cause of death as meningitis-cerebro-spinal epidemic. [8] When he contracted the disease was not listed, but his remains were shipped to College Point in a hermetically sealed coffin on May 8, 1919. [9]

Early studies released after the war seemed to indicate there was no definite relation between influenza and meningitis, [10] however in October 1918, the weekly bulletin of the American Expeditionary Forces in Europe documented a sharp rise in reports of cerebrospinal meningitis approximately one week after sharp increases in reports of influenza and pneumonia. The bulletin noted that "it has been a usual observation that when infections of the upper respiratory tract prevail, the incidence of meningitis in the community increases soon after, and this rule prevails at present."

During the same time period, there were historically high numbers and rates of meningococcal disease in U.S. civilian and military populations. In the U.S. Army, recruits in initial training camps and soldiers who had recently disembarked from troop ships, were at highest risk.[11]

Henry's remains were buried in Flushing Cemetery on May 11th. [10] With both parents deceased, family mourners would have included his sister Clara, and his brother William, both of whom were married, and raising families. His burial received no newspaper coverage, so it can only be hoped that full military honors were accorded.

While the last shot fired in anger had taken place in France on November 11th, the death of one more College Point man in service during the nineteen months of American involvement would be reported in the spring of 1919.

41

Arthur Kraemer

July 22, 1897 - May 9, 1919

Arthur Kraemer died one day less than six months after the last shot was fired ending World War One. Twenty-three months earlier, when he registered for the draft, he was working as a deck hand on the College Point and Manhattan Ferry. [1] Seven weeks later, he enlisted in the Regular Army, [2] but that decision may have come about as something of a Hobson's Choice, take it or leave it.

His great grandfather, Peter, and his two brothers, John and Philip, immigrated from Germany to the Williamsburg section of Brooklyn in the mid-1840's. There they worked in Conrad Poppenhusen's factory before moving to College Point. In the decades that followed, a number of family members became active in community life, and gotten very involved in a variety of successful enterprises. Arthur's father, Otto, married to Jennie

Cavanagh, worked many years in the rubber company. Together they raised a family of eight children, five daughters and three sons. Arthur was second to the youngest.

From the days of his youth, Arthur had made a number of seriously questionable decisions. When he was nine, he and three friends, ages thirteen through seventeen, took in a moving picture show in College Point. The hit of the film was a train wreck that prompted them to discuss creating one of their own. Since College Point had a railroad with tracks undergoing repair, they decided it would be a good idea. Replacement ties had been positioned along the line, a number of them near a sharp curve. It was here they placed a tie across the tracks. The engineer saw it, but due to the speed at which the train was traveling, he was unable to stop. The passengers felt the bump as the train passed over the tie. Fortunately, no injuries were sustained, but it was obvious an attempt had been made to cause mayhem. On a tip from the station agent, College Point detective John Kraemer apprehended the seventeen year-old. When questioned, he implicated the others including the policeman's distant cousin, Arthur. The four delinquents were turned over to Children's Society in the Flushing Police Precinct, and Kraemer was paroled in the custody of an unnamed sister. [3]

In the ensuing years, there were other newspaper reports of his participation in matters untoward, a crap game here an assault there, and it may have been one of the latter that led to his enlistment. Less than a week after America's entry into the war, Arthur and an accomplice were found guilty of robbery and assault. He was also charged with carrying a concealed weapon. The court considered the assault a particularly vicious one, and some of the judges were inclined to impose a severe sentence. An investigation was made before sentence was imposed, [4] and it is entirely reasonable to conclude that Arthur Kraemer was given the option of either going to jail or enlisting in the military.

Whether he was or wasn't given a choice is unknowable, but on March 16th the following year, Arthur Kraemer departed for Europe, a member of Company G, 3rd Ammunition Train, on board U.S. Army transport 509. [5] He saw action in the Second Battle of the Marne, Chateau

Thierry; St. Mihiel, Mt. Faucon, and the Argonne. Significant engagements all, he came through every one unscathed. [6] The 3rd Ammunition Train remained in France following the end of the war, and did not return to the United States until the following August. For Private 1st Class Arthur Kraemer it was a different story. At the end of February, he entered Base Hospital # 69 in the village of Savenay with what appeared to be influenza contracted while in the line of duty. Complications set in almost immediately, pleurisy followed by tubercular meningitis. [7]

"Savenay was a tuberculosis hospital where men diagnosed with the illness were cared for. If the soldier had even a fighting chance of being cured he was packed into the hospital ward of a ship and rushed home. If not, as in the case of Arthur Kraemer, Savenay was a cheery place. There were croquet and less strenuous games to play and broad piazzas that looked down across the valley toward the Loire River. Red Cross nurses came and went and did their best to comfort and amuse the soldiers and make them forget; forget the back door of the little hospital where night after night four or five fellows went out – in pine boxes, never to return, and the rows of wooden crosses down in the American cemetery at the foot of the hill steadily grew." [8] Arthur Kraemer died two months after admission, and was buried in Grave #335, Cemetery #22, "the one at the foot of the hill. [9]

While there is nothing in the burial file to indicate he had written home to inform his mother and family that he was ill, it seems as if he might have. In her letters written in response to three received from the government, Jennie Cavanaugh Kraemer expressed no sense of shock at the news of his having died. The first contained the news of her son's passing. She wrote an acknowledgment. Three months later, she penned a request for an update on when she could expect arrival of her son's body. She had dutifully responded to all government letters, and done everything directed. Still, she had no idea as to when his remains would be returned for burial in the family plot at Calvary Cemetery in nearby Woodside. [10]

Incredibly, a year went by with no word. On September 9th, she wrote once again. "I would be so glad to have his body sent home. I have looked for his body day by day. I have a grave of my own to receive him. I have notified the undertaker and made all the arrangements. Day after day and night after night it is on my mind that they might have sent his body to Hoboken and sent it to the National Cemetery and buried his body without notifying me about it. Will you please investigate this case? It is praying [*sic*] on my mind." [11]

The Army sent a telegram very soon thereafter advising the anxious mother that her son's body had arrived stateside aboard the U.S. Army transport *Sherman*. Once again Jennie Cavanaugh Kraemer wrote a reply, this one quite long. "It arrived home at 4 o'clock on the 17th, more joy for me than sorrow; my sadness seems to have left me." She then continued to elaborate on the involvement of the newly established American Legion Post 853, and their having sent a floral piece. She told of a Red Cross nurse who had attended him in France, a Brooklyn girl, who had visited her home. In addition to a copy of a newspaper article telling the story of the arrival and burial of Arthur Kraemer's body, she enclosed the 1920 Oscar Ammann Post 853 Memorial Day booklet. Arthur's picture was marked with an "X". She also enclosed a photograph of the home she was planning to buy using the proceeds from her son's War Risk Insurance. [12]

The Solemn Requiem Mass was held at St. Fidelis Church followed by interment at Calvary Cemetery. Acting as an honor guard was a detachment of troops from Fort Totten in full uniform, together with a firing squad. Also in attendance were members of the College Point branch of the American Red Cross, and the American Legion. [13]

Jennie Cavanaugh Kraemer died in 1923. [14] Following a Requiem Mass at St. Fidelis, she was buried in Calvary with her son. Otto Kraemer outlived her by two years, dying in Bellevue Hospital after a short illness. His death occurred over the Memorial Day weekend as College Point celebrated the holiday remembering those who had served, and those who had given their all. Funeral services were held at his late residence, the home purchased using Arthur's War Risk Insurance. Burial followed at Flushing Cemetery, and for reasons unknown, not at Calvary. [15]

It must be believed that whatever transgressions Arthur Kraemer committed in the days of his youth, were atoned for in France. Driving ammunition to the front lines every night was perilous duty. There were no dugouts in which to seek shelter. Driving on shell-torn roads through muck and mire peering into blackness carrying enough shells and powder to blow a regiment clear up to heaven's door was a race with death he and others relentlessly, but willingly endured. August Bigler lost his life by being blown to bits on an ammunition train in France. Arthur Kraemer contracted Influenza, and died slowly. There were no slackers on an Ammunition Train. [16]

Poppenhusen Institute

The Observor
Bas-Relief by Hermon Atkins MacNeil
For Victory Celebration

Guard Them - Lend Your Money
Bas-Relief by Hermon Atkins MacNeil
For Fourth Liberty Loan Drive

42

To Honor Fallen Heroes

College Point went wild over the peace news Thursday afternoon and evening. Steam whistles screeched, church bells rang and all factories closed down for the day. Automobiles loaded with enthusiastic occupants raced about, and a number of cheering crowds headed by drum corps and well supplied with noisemakers, paraded in the afternoon until late into the evening. There was only one problem, Thursday's date was November 7th, and the spontaneous outburst was based on an unsubtantiated report of the armistice having been signed. [1]

Four days later, the scene was repeated. Once again factories doors were shut tight, and the school children were dismissed. Early in the morning, the employees of the Kleinert Rubber Company started the day off with a parade. They were soon joined by workers from the other factories, along with children of the public schools, and St. Fidelis school as well. The same steam whistles hooted, and church bells rang out in celebration of the good news. [2]

Though they were up early enough to join in the celebrations, at the same time they had begun, twenty-two College Point men departed the village en route to Fort Totten. Uncle Sam had called, and they responded,[3] but their time in Uncle Sam's Army was limited to one night. All were instructed to return from whence they had come, but when the memorial was unveiled, their names were on it. At least two actually chose to serve, but when the remaining twenty were asked in the 1930 census if they had, all who could be found indicated they had not.

There were two parades in the evening. The Police Reserves, the Boy Scouts, and Girl Pioneers marched in one. They were followed by men, women and children from mere infants to gray-haired old folks, automobiles, trucks, and other vehicles. Some had been at it all day, but they kept up making as much noise as they could. [4] The Boy Scouts then led a parade of several thousand factory workers across the Causeway to Flushing where a huge celebration was underway. The war had finally come to an end. Besides the Boy Scouts band, there was music of every variety, horns, bells, tin pans, and every sort of a noise contrivance possible. [5]

Lasting into the early morning, the exhuberant jubilation subsided, people returned, as much as possible, to their routines, and two days later all the libraries in Queens reopened. They had been shut down temporarily due to the influenza epidemic, [6] a plague that had not truly run its course.

On Sunday, November 24th, days before America would celebrate Thanksgiving, another grand parade was held in the village. Despite biting winds and chilling temperatures, Civil War Veterans had the honor of leading the grand procession. Their numbers dwindling with every passing year, they rode comfortably in a single automobile. Behind them marched a group of enthusiastically received soldiers and sailors, followed by members of more than twenty village organizations. The seemingly endless column concluded at a speaker's stand. Reformed Church pastor Rev. Henry Sluyter opened the ceremonies with a fervent prayer for the welfare of the boys still in Europe, for their parents, and friends at home, and for the country. A large flag measuring 15' x 25' was then released to the breeze by Sergeant Charles Schreiner, representing the Army, and Walter Christensen, the Navy. As they were setting this scene, the College Point Mannerchor, the village's long established German singing society, along with the Marvin International Order of Odd Fellows Glee Club sang the "Star Spangled Banner." Poppenhusen Institute Principal John G. Embree accepted the flag on behalf of the town, and spoke with great feeling of the patriotism of College Point's sons. "The war is over, but our duty to those in service is not. When the boys come home we will have a great duty to perform - to welcome them, and help them, and give them proper recognition for the great work they have done." [7]

The flag, a white field bordered in red with the numerals "600" formed in blue stars, was suspended on a wire stretching across the town's main street. Eighteen gold stars representing those who had made the supreme sacrifice, were incorporated into the red border at the top. It was soon to be learned the number was greater than eighteen. Father Schumack concluded the exercises with a benediction. [8] It was indeed a memorable, emotion-filled day for all participants. Not a great many boys had as yet made it home from France and other points around the globe, but everyone was encouraged to keep the home fires burning in anticipation of that long hoped-for day.

As far back as early September, a committee had already announced plans to erect a temporary memorial when the end of a war was yet a dream. The Poppenhusen's John G. Embree had assembled and published 572 names for inclusion, one of them his son, John Harold. [9] No indication of what form the honor roll would take was provided, but the preferred site was a small 19' x 200' swath of land fronting on the railroad station. Before the war, its salad days long past, the area had become a dumping ground, a genuine community eyesore. To rectify the situation, Embree also undertook the task of forming a committee to restore the area in preparation for an upcoming, 4th of July celebration. Sculptor Hermon MacNeil had earlier spoken on how easy it would be to turn the area into a place of beauty through the addition of trees, shrubbery, and a flag pole. [10] His suggestions and those of others were implemented, and on that glorious day, bands played, patriotic songs were sung, and speeches were made. The festivities came to a close with the raising of a handsome flag to the top of a newly installed pole. A detail of soldiers from Fort Totten gave a salute, joined by a chorus of school children singing the "Star Spangled Banner." [11]

After the November 11th celebrations and parades had passed into history, an early February report indicated work was progressing on College Point's memorial tablet. Six hundred and ten names, arranged alphabetically, had already been inscribed. Six of the names were young women. It would soon be ready for dedication. [12] There was no indication as to whether or not this was the result of Embree's effort, but the likelihood is that it was.

College Point's Honor Roll was unveiled on the morning of February 25th in what became known as Memorial Square in front of the railroad station. [13] Two large metal tablets measuring 4' x 6', were suspended on the cross arms fastened to the flagpole, and surmounted by a shield of the American colors. Across the tops of the tablets were the gold-lettered words, College Point's Sons - Who Answered The Call - To Make the World - Safe For Democracy.

Below each phrase, on both sides of the tablets, were the names of what was believed to be a final total of 627 young men, and seven young women who had served their country. Gold stars appeared opposite the names of the young heroes who had made the supreme sacrifice, and those who had willingly served their country in the Army, Navy, Marine Corps, and Merchant Marine. Arranged alphabetically, the names included neither branch of service nor rank.

Of the women whose names were listed, six served in the Navy as Yeomen, Amelia Brenneis, Marjorie Cooney, Eunice Champlain Dawson, Emily Hetzer, Marie Anna Walters and Louise Marie Wolfe [14] A seventh, Cora Hanson, became a registered nurse. Not included was Josephine Seitz, who also served in the Navy. Though his family had a long history in the village, Ernest B. Plitt's name was also not listed. Countless communities across the vast expanse of the United States were planning memorials. Characteristically, College Point was among the first to get it done. From the very beginning, the expectation was that this memorial was not going to be permanent.

College Point's Sons Who Answered the Call

To Make the World Safe For Democracy

One year and one week after the armistice was signed, the permanent memorial question was discussed at a well-attended meeting held at the Poppenhusen Institute. It was hoped that plans for raising funds would be finalized without delay. [15] A committee was formed, chaired by Rev. Benjamin Mottram. Working alongside him were Rev. Henry Sluyter from the Reformed Church, and John G. Embree. [16]

Mottram sent a letter to all College Point citizens, organizations and schools, soliciting ideas as to what form the memorial should take? He asked responders to consider where it should be located, its size and dimensions, what it should embody, the purpose it should serve and the probable cost of erection and maintenance. [17] A sub-committeee had also been formed to get the youth of the community involved, by way of a contest. Cash prizes would be awarded to students for the best ideas submitted in the form of a composition. [18]

Many suggestions came forth. They ranged from erecting a monument to the dead, to one for both the living and the dead. Others proposed constructing a building in their memory to be used for community gatherings and activities. Still others recommended giving monetary rewards to those who had left the work of their youth to enter the service. The student response was substantial, generating almost five hundred compositions. About three hundred were present at the Poppenhusen Institute when selections were made. Only a small percentage received awards, but their showing was as indicative of the spirit in College Point, as was that demonstrated by the entire community. [19]

While it was reasonable to expect that sculptor Hermon Atkins MacNeil would have been enjoined to lend his prodigious talents to the project, it did not happen. He and Embree had a friendship going back to 1907, when MacNeil had been charged with finding a replacement for the suddenly deceased, Poppenhusen Institute Director. The search resulted in Embree being hired for the much coveted position, the Institute being highly regarded for the quality of its education program. It is unknown whether or not the famed sculptor, an authority on war memorials, was invited to participate. If he was, out of necessity, he probably declined. Early in January 1920, he was on his way to Rome, and not scheduled to return until mid-year. [20] The expectation was that the project would have been finalized by then. It was not. Instead, there was little progess. MacNeil accepted a commission in 1924 to commemorate the soldiers and sailors from Flushing, seventy in all, who had laid down their lives in service to their country. That neighboring village's memorial was dedicated in 1925. [21] One year later, College Point's honor boards were given a fresh coat of paint, the names of those who had given their lives shining anew. [22]

Five more years would pass before College Point dedicated its permanent memorial replacing the two metal tablets that had graced the Memorial Square flagpole for more than a decade. In moving exercises held on May 30th, a few weeks before embarking for France on the Pilgrimage for War Mothers and Widows, Mrs. Paula Ammann accepted a bronze plaque on behalf of the community, in memory of the College Point men who had died in service. [23] There were more than a thousand persons marching in the parade that preceded the ceremonies. They included members of the American Legion Post named in honor of her son on Memorial Day eleven years earlier. Also taking part were other Gold Star Mothers, Spanish-American War veterans, members of the Odd Fellows Lodge, the Boy's Band, Boy and Girl Scout troops, and children from the community's public and parochial schools. [24] As an added touch to the exercises, some of the local school students released a large number of homing pigeons. [25] On Armistice Day, November 11th, the plaque, elegant in its simplicity and affixed to a marble base, was dedicated in Memorial Square.

Only twenty names appeared. More accurately, there should have been twenty-eight. Missing were George Rauh, James J, Powers, Ernest B. Plitt, Stephen Melbourne Schwab, Hyman Lashiwer, Louis Fritz, Henry Zimmer, and Arthur Kraemer.

These were ordinary men who lived during extraordinary times. They accomplished noteworthy things in the course of their abbreviated lives if serving and dying for their country counts as being noteworthy. It is precisely because their lives were ordinary that their stories were told. It is not the number of years of life that brings honor rather it is the quality of those years. By their service and sacrifice, these men deserve to have told the stories of their valiant deeds, and in so doing honor fallen heroes. We, those who have benefited by their actions, weep with all who bore, and bear their unbearable loss.

COLLEGE POINT'S SONS

John Abbate
William M. Aha*
Thomas Aird
Henry W. Altman
Michael Amberg
Oscar Ammann †
Arthur Anderson
Gilbert Andrews
Kurt Angenbroich
Basilio Apostolon
Edward Huntington Arne*
Bernard Arons
Louis Asfar
Frank W. Baacke
William Balzer
Joseph Baluk
William Balzer
Robert H. Banker
William F. Baresch
Edward J. Barrett
George Barrett
Harold Barrett
John Barrett
Joseph Barrett
John A. Barth
Joseph P. Barthel*
William Barthel
Harold V. Bartholomew
Raymond S. Barto
John B. Battle
Fred Bauer
Godfrey Bauer, Jr.
John J. Bauer
William Baumeister
Frank J. Baumert
William R. Baumert, Jr.
Fred Baumgartner*
Lewis Bautz
Frederick Beaver
Max G. Beck
John Becker
Joseph Becker
Charles Behnstedt
Hal Benedict
Harold Bennison
Albert Berchtold
Charles Beresheim
Joseph Beresheim, Jr.
Arthur Bergauer
Charles Bertschinger
Harry M. Biffar
August Bigler †
Jacob Bigler
George Birkle
Frederick Baumgartner
Charles Blaeser
Joseph Blasi

Walter Blanck
Casper Blass
Benjamin F. Blue †
Johan F. Bobst
Emil Boehm
Alfred J. Boller
Charles H. Boller
Ray C. Bonjour
John F. Bopp
Charles Bornemann
Herman Bornemann, Jr.
Bshar Boyajy
Frank G. Braun
David Breen
Henry M. Breen*
August W. Breisacher †
Fred Breisacher
Leonard Bridge
George Brill
Rudolph Brugger †
Edwin Brunswick
John Buckholtz
Fred Buerger
William E. Buerger †
Louis Buettel
Louis Buhl
Theo A. Buhl
Frank Busch
James Butler
Charles M. Bux
George Bux
John J. Byrnes*
Frank Campbell
Lorenzo Capone
Frank W. Carroll*
Clifford C. Carroll
John Carroll
Jack Champlain
Charles Chandler
Alexander Chodos
Walter L. Chrestesen
John K. Chopian
Edward Clair
George Clark
Joseph Connor
Vincent Connor
Clarence Connors
Jerome C. Connors
Michael Connors
Eugene J. Cooney
James Cooney
Peter Cooney
Thomas P. Cooney
Christopher Cooney*
Michael Corcoran
Joseph H. Corey
Michael Cosgrave

Christian J. Coyne
Paul Crecelius
John Creeden
John Cregan
William Crook
Edward Cummings
Lorenzo Capone
Valentine Darius
Joseph L. Dartley
Edward Davis
Abbot A. Day
Allen Deakin
William Delamain
Frank Delaney
John J. Delaney
Fred J. DeLisle
Harry J. Devine
Frank J. Devlin
Nick DiBennedetto
Charles Diehr
George M. Diehr
George Dietz
Hale Diller
Fred Dillmann
Henry Dillmann, Jr.
Alfred J. Dillon
Joseph M. Dillon
John Dobrinsky
Albert Dockendorf
Arthur K. Doebele
Fred Doerr
Louis Doerr †
Killian Doerr
Daniel Donaldson*
Ambrose Donnelly
George Dono
Henry Dono
Edward T. Doran
James F. Doran
Joseph Doran
Edward Dougherty
William H. J. Down
Edgar Downie
John R. Downie
Charles S. DuBois
George M. Duer
Carl Duesselmann
Gregory O. Dvorak
Henry Eberhard
Joseph P. Ehatt
George Ehrlich
Benjamin H. Earl*
Alfred Eisenacht
George C. Eisenacht
John Ellison
John H. Embree †
John B. Endres †

WHO ANSWERED THE CALL

Joseph Engle*
John Englehardt
Arthur G. English
Charles Eppenbach
Edwin Eppenbach
Louis Evers
John Fagan
Thomas Fagan †
Alfred Falvey
Santo Fernandez
George Field
John Fink
William Ambrose Flanigan*
Fred S. Folger
Leo R. Ford
Alfred Frank
Edward Frank
Emil L. Franke
Edward Frankenstein
Floyd Frankenstein
Albert W. Frey †
Charles Freygang
Harry W. Frick
Leroy Frick
Max Fricke
Albert Friedmann
Percy Friedmann
Louis George Fritz †
Fred Folger*
Alfred Ganss
Henry L. Ganss
Walter Ganss
Walter Garvin
Jacob Geib
Alfred Geidel
Christian Geidel †
George Georgiadis
Theodore Geraldi*
Herbert E. Geres
Frederick J. Gerhart*
John L. Gerhardt
Morris Gessner*
Frank Gibney
George E. Gillette
Joseph Giordino
Charles Globe
Albert Golsner
Frank Golsner
Fred Golsner
Anthony Gordon*
William L. Grace
Charles Graeser
Edward P. Graeser
George Gray
William Greb
Gustave Greiner
Louis J. Greiner

George D. Griffin
Harry Griffin
Carlo Grimaldi
George Grimm*
Louis Grossfeld
Richard F. Guest
Gustave Gugliucci
Frank Guido
Thomas J. Gunson
Albert Haas
Charles Hachtel
Fred Hachtel
Charles F. Haenggi
Ambrose Haering
John Hamburger
Fred Hanky
Ludwig Harjes
Francis Harper
Elson Harter
Clarence Hartmann
William Harvey
George Hauck
Philip H. Hauseman
Stephen Hauseman
George M. Hawkens
Charles J. Heck
Fred Heck
Richard Heidenreich
Jacob Philip Heinrich
George Hemrick
Herman Hengge
Frank Henrich
Henry Heitink, Jr.
William. G. Hoenig
William. G. Hoffer
Charles. Hoffmann
George Hoffmann
Henry Hoffmann
Jacob Hoffmann
William Hoffmann
Harry Hollister
Arthur Hollweg
Herman Hollweg
Louis Hollweg
Leon V. Holmes
Christos Hondropolos*
Fred Hook
Manuel Hook
Clarence Horn
Edward M. Horn
Nicholas Howlett
Charles M. Huber
Paul Hubert
Francis X. Hulser
Jerome W. Hulser
Albert Humm
Edwin Humm

Arthur Humm
John J. Huston
William Huston
Walter A. Ilch
Charles A. Jacob
Raymond W. Jacob
Anthony Jeanette
Gustav C. Jockers
William F. Jockers*
Arthur F. Johnson*
Harry Kazakeris
Jerome Kalehos
William B. Kalwiss
Denis Kaphezezis
Charles Kaufman
William Kaufman
Henry D. Kellermann
John Kellerman
Fred Kirschner
Otto Kirschner
Albert Kirsch
Jacob Klahr
Ernest G. Klein
Joseph H. Kline
Leopold Klinger
Frank J. Klinker
Leo Klumpen
William Klumpen
Henry F. Knetter
Arthur Koch
George F. Koch
Harry Koerper
Herman Koll
Harry Kollmer
Arthur Kraemer †
Frank H. Kraemer
Walter W. Kraemer
Adolph E. Kress
Fred Kruser
Charles Kullman
William Kunst
Max Louis Kurtz*
William Kussman
Anthony Labella
Hyman Lashiwer †
Edward Lane
Herbert J. Latz
William J. Latz
Joseph F. Lauda
James A. Leaman
John Lehman
George F. Lenhardt*
Herman G. Lerner
John P. Lerner
Harry E. Lewis
William J. Lewis
Meyer Lobsenz

TO MAKE THE WORLD

Peter Locke
Arthur J. Lorbecker*
Philip Lorbecker
William Lorbecker
Otino Loreto
Joseph Lorkowski
John Lotz
George F. Lutz
George MacPherson
Herman J. Maeurer
Benjamin Magid
John F. Maher
Charles O. Mahler †
Henry Mahler
Joseph Mahoney
William Mahoney
William E. Mainz
Fred E. Mann
Nicholas Marchese
Frank Marino
Andrew Marky
Jacob Marky
Edward Martin
Joseph Martin
Thomas J. Martin
Albert Martini
Louis Martini
Charles Marx
Earlue Mason
Charles Maurer
John McCormick
Thomas McCormick †
Clarence McCracken
William McCrooks*
James McGivney
Patrick McKenna
Thomas McMahon
Paul McMichael
Frank Meier
William Meier*
Jacob Melder
Nicholas Menth*
Anthony Merkle
Edward Merkle
Harry Merkle
George Merkle
Charles Messbauer
John Messbauer
George Metz
Edward W. Michel
Frank J. Michel
Harry Francis Michel*
Harry W. Michaels
Alfred Middlebrook
Charles Miller
Melville Miller
George Misack*

Andrew Moakley
William Mohrmann †
Joseph Molitor
Paul Monroe
Alexander Morris
James Morrison
John P. Motz
Philip Motz
William L. Mount*
Albert Mueller
George Mueller*
William E. Mueller
Frank J. Muller
William J. Muller*
Edward Muller
William Mueller
Maurice Nash
James Neely
Richard A. Neely
Arthur E. Nelson
Herman Newnom
John W. Newnom Jr.
Harry B. Newman
Otto G. Nordman
Charles Nostrand
Edward P. Oberlies
George J. Oberlies
Thomas F. O'Reilly
William F. Orgass
Howard G. Orgass
Edward T. O'Rourke
Fred Ortenberg
Nicholas Orth
Fred Otten
Ernest Otto
Henry Otto
Albert Palmer
Ray T. Palmer
Peter Papalexis*
William Cyril Pauly
Ernest Arthur Payne
Charles Peck
Harry Personik
Peter Pickel
Ernest B. Plitt* †
Edward Poll
Andrew Poremba
Charles Pores
Dan Pores
Charles Posthauer, Jr.
James Powers †
Howard R. Prichard
John F. Prost
August Prostler
Bartholomew F. Prostler
George J. Prostler
Thomas J. Prostler

William Prostler*
Howard R. Pugsley
William J. Quaid
Charles F. Quaid
Wilfred Quick
John Rabasco
George Rauh †
Charles Rausch
Frank Rausch
Robert J. Rausch
Louis Rauchenberger
Christian Regelman
Emil Reindell
Andrew Reinhardt
Jacob Reinhardt
Joseph Reinhardt
John J. Reul
George A. Reyl
Herbert Riecker
Adolph Robert
Frank Robinson
Alfred Rocklein
John Rocklein
Joseph Rocklein
Fred Rodgers
William Rodgers, Jr.
John O. Roesch
Arthur B. Rooney †
Clarence Roszel
Henry Christian Roth *
Charles Ruckdaschel
Otto Rueggeberg
Charles Rumenapp
Albert Rusch
Charles Ryan
Gustav Rymski
Robert S. Saunders
Charles Saxtorph
Edward Sayer
John Sayer
Walter Schaad
John Schaefer*
Charles Schank
Gustav Schauer
Joseph Schatt
Alfred Schlesinger
Charles L. F. Schmeltz
Fred W. Schmidt
Leonard Schmidt
Louis Schmidt †
Fred Schmidt
Valentine Schmidt*
Emil Schnell
George F. Schnurer
William Schoenfeld
Julius A. Schomber
Frank Schreiber

SAFE FOR DEMOCRACY

Charles Schreiner
Fred Schreiner
Charles Schultheis
Daniel Schultheis
Henry Schultheis
William Schultheis
Irving Schultz
Frank Schuman
Andrew J. Schwab
Emil J. Schwab †
Stephen M. Schwab †
Gohmann Seacat
John Sebold
Ernest Seering*
Carl E. Seip
Louis Senger
Henry Seuffert
Franklin Shuart*
Martin Shuart
Harry Siegenthal
Gustave Siegrist
Joseph Sienkovo
Charles Simon
William R. Siena*
Fred Simpson
Arthur Skelly
William Slater
Thomas Smart
Harry Smith
James Smith
Vincent W. Smith
Raymond J. Smyth*
Herman Solomon
Adolph Sonnenthal
Fred Souder
Joseph W. Soukop
George A. Spaeth
William Sperling
Charles Stack
Edward Stack †
Thomas Stack
Herman Staffeldt*
Clarence E. Stantial
Theodore Stark
Carl Steffen
Walter C. Steffen*
Anthony Steiger
Henry Steiger
Joseph Steiger
Edward J. Steinbrenner
Joseph G. Steinbrenner
William H. Steinbrenner
Otto Steinbrenner
Alvah Steiner
Alfred Edwin Steiner
George Steiner
Alfred Stengel †

Charles Stengel
Charles Stephany
George S. Stiles
John L. Stockinger
William G. Stockinger
Frederick Stouke
Martine Stouke
Edward Straube, Jr.
Joseph. L. Stother
Howard W. Stumpf
Fred Sulzbach
Joseph Sulzbach
Eugene Sweeney
Alexander Szita
Elliott G. Szita
Max Tanz
Fred Tewes
Arne C. Thine
J. F. Thom
William Thorogood
Eugene Tonns
Bryant Tracy
Harry Tracy
Lawrence Trimble
Henry Troesch
Alexander Trzaska
Stanley Trzaska
George Tuffin
William Tuffin
Fred Tyler
Charles Unbekant
Leonard Unverzagt
Bernard Vaas
Harry Vaas
Joseph Vokans
Carl Von Sothen
Rudolph Voyteck
William Wagner
Otto Wahl
John Wainwright
William Waltrop
Albert Watt
August G. Weber
Joseph Weinzettle
Charles Weiss
Victor Werscher
Frank Weth
Edward White
Richard White
Jacob Wick
George Wiedmann
William Wiegand
Joseph Wilhelm
Harold B. Wilkinson
George Williams
Richard Ambrose Williams*
Robert V. Williams

Henry Will
Henry Willows
Joseph Andrew Wilson
Joseph Winkler
Edward Winter
John Winters
Herbert Witzel
Joseph Witzel
Louis Woelke
Henry Woerner
Charles Wohlmacher
Edward Wohlmacher
Otto Wolbert
Edward Wolf
Charles Wolf
Albert Wohlfarth
Morris Wolinsky
Philip Wolinsky
Joseph Wolinsky*
Robert W. Wood
Charles F. Wurtz
Henry Zimmer †
Kenneth Zoeller
Martin Zwicke
Adolph J. Zwilinski
Herman S. Zwilinski

Total: 653 Men

Amelia Brenneis
Marjorie Cooney
Eunice G. Dawson
Emily C. Hetzer
Marie Walters
Louise Wolfe
Cora Hanson

* Not on Original Memorial
† Died During War

Epilogue

American Legion Post #853 was established on Memorial Day 1920. One year earlier, with war memories still fresh, over four hundred men, every one a veteran, had convened at the Poppenhusen Institute. They had come together to discuss establishing a support organization for all those who had served in the war. They also wanted to set aside a place where they could meet to talk over their experiences, and share stories over a glass of beer. [1] That would have been difficult to do. Prohibition had gone into effect on January 17th with the passage of the Eighteenth Amendment. It would be the law of the land for the next thirteen years.

The organization was to be called "College Point Veterans of the World War", and like all other things done in this little town, this organization happened to be one of the first of its kind in the country. At this time, veterans from all the states were establishing similar organizations. From this groundswell, the Congress of the United States chartered the American Legion. According to charter rules, only fifteen to twenty individuals could form a post. These founders could subsequently invite others to join. With over five hundred veterans signing on, College Point's petition created a problem for the national organization; how to accommodate such a large number of veterans wishing to form a post. Perseverance won the crown. As a result of pressure applied, a special ruling was set in place, and the post was established without incident. At a subsequent meeting held at the Institute, a unanimous decision was made to name the Post in honor of Oscar Ammann, held in memory as the first man from College Point to be officially recognized as having been killed in action. [2]

With an estimated population of 16,000 in 1920, post-war College Point had remained a good place to live and work. Even though war-related government contracts had long been cancelled, it was still recognized as being second only to Long Island City as an industrial center. According to *Queens Borough: The Borough of Homes and Industry*, the official organ of the Queens Chamber of Commerce, more than three thousand men and women were employed in the village's factories, thirteen of them large, and eighteen, small. One thousand people worked at John W. Rapp's Empire Art Metal Products. The American Hard Rubber Company employed almost seven hundred, Kleinert's Rubber factory, over five hunded, and the Myhnepo Silk Mills, over three hundred. Weapons manufacturer Victor R. Browning Company had moved out. Beacon Falls Rubber Shoe Company, and the Top Notch Shoe Company soon followed. In short order, the shoe-making industry in College Point was history. The College Point Boat Corporation had launched its last submarine chaser in 1919. George Stelz, it was thought, would go back to building pleasure craft. Approaching age sixty in 1930, he listed his occupation as carpenter in that year's census. There was no mention of boats, the business having ceased doing business in the mid-1920s.

Rapp died in 1922 bringing about the closure of Empire Art Metal. Less than two years later, L.W.F. Engineering was forced to shut down due to what was characterized as general depression in the aircraft industry. [3] The last aircraft made by the company flew over the College Point on April 16, 1924. It was a seaplane destined for the U.S. Navy. [4] A severe blow was dealt to the airplane manufacturing industry at large, and to College Point in particular. But right on the heels of its failure, a revival took hold when three companies, Edo Aircraft Corporation, Sikorsky Aero Engineering Company, and Aero Supply Corporation, moved in. [5] Edo's name was formed using the initials of its founder, Earl Dodge Osborne. Sikorsky was a renowned aviation pioneer who had built his first helicopter in 1908. [6] Aero Supply manufactured airplane hardware and accessories. [7] To meet what was perceived as an educational need to be filled, the Poppenhusen Institute planned to offer free aviation courses, [8] but by 1930, two of the three firms were gone. Aero Supply moved from its factory on 15th Avenue and 132nd Street to Dayton, Ohio; [9] Sikorsky, from the buildings formerly occupied by L.W. F. engineering, to Bridgeport, Connecticut. [10] Edo stayed, and still operates at the same location at the foot of 14th Avenue at the water's edge. Additional companies had opened up for business such that the village thrived, even in the early days of the Depression. [11]

The end came for Ambrose Schumack on December 28, 1930. [12] He died almost forty-two years to the day of his arrival in College Point. Universally loved and recognized, his passing was mourned by people of all faiths, not only in College Point, but also throughout New York City. He was buried in the St. Fidelis churchyard.

Not long thereafter, on August 24, 1932, August Ebendick, pastor of St. John's Lutheran Church since Civil War days, took his last breath. [13] He had come to the community in 1864, served well his congregation over a span of forty-six years, and retired in 1910. He was 94. The church prospered with the man who took his place, Pastor Arthur Halfmann, especially during the war years. Throughout the course of his ministry, he vitalized the church in many ways, and was happily remembered for having played both piano and organ at numberless church, and community functions. He died in April 1938 at age 61. [14]

Rev. Henry Sluyter passed away in New Jersey in 1940. [15] He was 67. After leaving College Point in 1921, he became pastor of the Second Reformed Church in Paterson, New Jersey. He served that congregation until his death. Having graduated from Hope College in Holland, Michigan in 1899, three decades later the school conferred upon him a Doctor of Divinity degree. Before coming to College Point, he had worked among Indian tribes in Oklahoma, and also served a parish in Anchorage, Kentucky.

The name Benjamin Mottram was revered in St. Paul's Episcopal Church. He remarried in 1925, served the parish until his retirement in 1956, and died on August 8, 1960. [16]

Nineteen veterans passed away in the decade that followed the end of the war. [17] Some were the result of things known like the lingering effects of influenza. Others died from natural causes, and one veteran took his own life. Newspaper reports indicated there were family issues that contributed to his action that were not connected to his service. [18] No matter the cause, his death cast a pall over the community.

Sailor William H. Delamain did not die during the war, but in March 1920 his death was the lead story in the nation's newspapers. He was the grandson of Henry Delamain, who since 1872 had been deeply involved in educating the village's children, and before his retirement, had been principal of all the College Point schools. Born in 1901, William was too young to join any branch of the military without his mother's consent. Regardless, he misrepresented his age, and in July 1918, enlisted in the Navy. [19] His first tour of duty expired in July 1920. He returned to College Point until September, then reenlisted, and volunteered for submarine duty. It was a fateful decision. Six months later, the boat on which he was serving ran aground off Santa Margarita Island as it approached the entrance to Magdalena Bay, Mexico. Four crewmen died. One of them was William Henry Delamain. College Point mourned another loss.[20]

Acknowledging some exceptions, in the final analysis it can be said that College Point had probably lost much of its culturally German character in the years leading up to the start of World War Two. Newspapers at the time made reference to its Prussian past, but no longer questioned its potential for disloyalty. The fact of its German roots was simply a matter of history. While industry still lines a portion of College Point's shoreline, buildings that once housed factories now contain penthouse condos. Undeveloped waterfront properties that in former times were seaweed-covered graveyards for cement barrels, or sandy beaches, have been extended out beyond those shores, and buttressed to support condominium townhouses.

As in most Queens Borough communities, the demographics have changed, and currently reflect greater diversity than that of the early decades of the 20th century. The annual Memorial Day parade is still held to commemorate, and venerate the memory of the men and women who have continued to safeguard America, and the rifle volleys continue to ring out salutes at the Memorial that took more than a decade to erect. In a letter to the Oscar Amman Post in early 1930, Father Francis Duffy wrote, "Oscar Ammann met his death like a hero. He was killed by a rifle bullet, indicating he had climbed to the top of the trench in defense of his sector. He was a good soldier, and a good man." [21] Nothing else needed to be said.

From data available today that may not have been known in late 1918, the original number of names of men who served was increased from 627 to at least 653, but the exact number of College Point men who were drafted into the army, or enlisted in the nation's armed forces during World War One will probably never be known. Military Service Records, and other verifiable sources indicate that at minimum, 319 men were inducted into the National Army; an additional 86 enlisted, and 36 more joined the National Guard. The U. S. Naval Reserve enrolled 96 men, and 59 chose the U. S. Navy. 10 joined the U.S. Marine Corps, while 14 served in the Merchant Marine bringing the total number to 620. Of those who served in the Army, at least 36 suffered wounds in France. A number of them were gassed. From Service Records, a minimum 237 went overseas, and more than 177 filled various positions stateside. It is probable that all who went into the Merchant Marine faced the possibility of being torpedoed, and all probably spent time in Europe. As far as it can be determined, none of the men who joined the Navy or Naval Reserve fought in France, but ships on which many of them served, crossed the Atlantic filling a variety of roles that included convoy escort. According to extant records, none of the ten Marines saw duty in Europe.

From its inception, the reason for writing this book was to honor, not only those men who lost their lives in the war, but all of College Point's heroes, to put flesh to bone on the men whose names are commemorated on the Eighteenth Avenue monument, and to those whose names were somehow omitted. College Point may not be as German as it once was, but it is still, at least in memory, a small German-American community seven and a half miles from the heart of New York City whose sons answered the call to make the world safe for democracy.

Endnotes

June 5, 1917

1. Keegan, John. *The First World War*, Alfred A. Knopf: New York, 1999.

2. *Flushing Daily Times*, "Conscription A Huge Success", June 6,1917.

3. ibid.

4. *Flushing Daily Times*, "3,687 Registered In Third Ward", June 7, 1917.

5. *Flushing Daily Times*, "Government Warns All Who Must Register", June 4, 1917.

6. *Flushing Daily Times*, "Millions Will Escape Draft," July 3, 1917

7. *Daily Star,* "Citizens Co-Operate In Getting Recruits", April 9, 1917.

8. *Daily Star*, "To Launch Naval Reserve Movement At College Point", April 21, 1917.

9. Trippett, Josephine, Naval Reserve Nurse, *Sketch of a Naval Emergency Hospital*, The American Journal of Nursing, 1918.

Conrad Poppenhusen

Haas, James E. *Conrad Poppenhusen: The Life of a German-American Industrial Pioneer*, Gateway Press: Baltimore, MD 2002.

Silk

1. *Brooklyn Daily Eagle*, "Timely Topics", May 26, 1882.

2. *The Newtown Register*, "Personal Notes", September 16, 1897.

3. *The Long Island Traveler*, "News Notes", March 9, 1883.

4. *The Newtown Register*, "Mr. Jacob Sulzbach", May 26, 1887.

5. *New York Times*, "Failures in Business", May 18, 1890.

6. *New York Times*, "Silk Manufacturers Fail", December 18, 1890.

7. *Brooklyn Daily Eagle*, "Silk Mills Strike Ended", October 27, 1897.

8. *New York Times*, "Silk Mill Closes at College Point", July 16, 1899.

9. *The Newtown Register*, July 20, 1899.

10. *Brooklyn Daily Eagle*, "Rhenania Silk Mills Sold", January 11, 1901.

11. *Brooklyn Daily Eagle*, "Hugo Funke", September 13, 1902.

12. *Brooklyn Daily Eagle*, "May Open Rhenania Mills", October 16, 1902.

13. *Brooklyn Daily Eagle*, "College Point Prosperous", November 7, 1902.

14. *New York Times*, "Silk Manufacturers Fail", December 18, 1890.

15. *Brooklyn Daily Eagle*, "Popular Flourishing Town On Long Island", January 18, 1880.

16. *Brooklyn Daily Eagle*, "City Over Blackwell's Island", April 16, 1899.

17. *Brooklyn Daily Eagle*, "College Point's New Industry", December 13, 1901.

18. http://shipbuildinghistory.com

Beer, Breweries & Gemütlichkeit

1. *Newtown Register*, December 30, 1875.

2. *New York Times*, April 28, 1887.

3. *New York Times*, "Business Troubles", June 15, 1893.

4. *Newtown Register*, Long Island Improvements and Industries", July 7, 1892.

5. *Evening Telegram*, "Asks For A Receiver", June 23, 1893.

6. *Brooklyn Daily Eagle*, "College Point Notes", October 8, 1896.

7. *Brooklyn Daily Eagle*, "New of Queensborough", April 25, 1899.

8. *Brooklyn Daily Eagle*, "Strikers Issue A Circular", April 29, 1899.

9. *Brooklyn Daily Eagle*, "Big Brewery Sold", July 6, 1910.

10. *New York Daily Tribune*, "On Long Island", July 5, 1871.

11. *Brooklyn Daily Eagle*, "Married Fifty Years", August 30, 1909.

12. *The New York Sun*, "College Point's Gala Day", October 7, 1883.

13. *New York Times*, "The Germantown Anniversary", October 7, 1883.

14. ibid. "College Point's Gala Day"

15. *Brooklyn Daily Eagle*, "Strikers Issue A Circular", April 29, 1899.

16. *Brooklyn Daily Eagle*, "No More Troubles Feared", April 26, 1899.

17. http://www.worldlingo.com/ma/enwiki/en/Glen_Island.

18. *The Evening Telegram*, March 26, 1887.

19. *Brooklyn Daily Eagle*, "College Point Catholics Generous", September 25, 1906.

20. *Brooklyn Daily Eagle*, "J.M. Donnelly's Will Proved", January 4, 1907.

21. *Brooklyn Daily Eagle*, "207 New Queens Buildings", June 19, 1916.

22. *New York Times*, "Realty Syndicate Buys Picnic Grove", January 20, 1926.

1900 - 1913

1. *Brooklyn Daily Eagle*, "Queens Borough Schools", May 16, 1900.

2. *New York Times*, "In Arms For The Lord's Prayer", January 28, 1885.

3. *Brooklyn Daily Eagle*, "Want German Taught", November 23, 1902.

4. ibid. "In Arms For The Lord's Prayer"

5. *Brooklyn Daily Eagle*, "German in Public Schools", October 7, 1901.

6. *Brooklyn Daily Eagle*, "Austrian Baronetcy for Long Island Priest", May 30, 1908.

7. *Brooklyn Daily Eagle*, "Resent Retirement of Their Aged Pastor", May 25, 1910.

1914 - 1916

1. *Brooklyn Daily Eagle*, "German Patriotic Aid Society", August 4, 1870.

2. *New York Times*, "Long Island", May 30, 1871.

3. *Daily Star*, "Marooned In Europe", August 3, 1914.

4. *Brooklyn Daily Eagle*, "War Rally Here By German-Americans", September 28, 1914.

5. *New Yorker Staats Zeitung*, "Thanksgiving Calls Up Patriotic Sentiments", November 26, 1914.

6. *Brooklyn Daily Eagle*, "In German Circles", March 11, 1915.

7. *Daily Star*, "A College Point Victim", May 13, 1915.

8. *Brooklyn Daily Eagle*, "$1,000,000 War Order No Lure to J. W. Rapp", June 18, 1915.

9. *Brooklyn Daily Eagle*, "Queens, Hive of Industry, Under the New City Plan", April 9, 1916.

10. *New York Times*, "Many New Factory Buildings Erected", May 15, 1915.

11. *Brooklyn Daily Eagle*, "Big Factory Deals at College Point", March 16, 1916.

12. *The Daily Long Island*, "$125,000 Factory Sale", February 15, 1916.

13. *Brooklyn Daily Eagle*, "207 New Queens Buildings", June 19, 1916.

14. *Daily Star*, "Aeroplane Factory Moves to College Point", July 21, 1916.

15. *Brooklyn Daily Eagle*, "Lease College Point Plant", July 21, 1916.

16. *New York Times*, "Many New Factory Buildings Erected", May 15, 1915.

17. *Washington Post*, "Contracts to be Let for Thirty Machines for the Navy", September 6, 1919.

18. *Washington Post*, "Seven Aeroplane Contracts", July 9, 1916.

Call to War

1. Keegan, John, *The First World War:* Alfred A. Knopf, New York, 1999.

2. *Brooklyn Daily Eagle*, "Says German-Americans Will Help to Preserve Nation", March 5, 1917.

3. *Newtown Register*, "German Sociability", May 3, 1888.

4. Author's analysis of 1860 and subsequent census records.

5. *New York Times*, "15 Men Died On The Vigilancia", March 20, 1917.

6. *New York Times*, "Ellis Island Life Easy for Germans", April 15, 1917.

7. *Flushing Daily Times*, "Rev. Father Schumack Tells German-Americans They Must Be Loyal", April 16, 1917.

8. *New York Times*, "Asks Germans to Enlist", April 16, 1917.

9. *Brooklyn Daily Eagle*, "Bars Alien Germans From Armory Zones", May 17, 1917.

10. ibid.

11. *New York Evening Telegram*, "50,000 Aliens Seek Permits in Barred Zones", May 29, 1917.

12. *Daily Star*, "To Build Submarine Chasers In College Point", May 20, 1917.

13. *Daily Star*, "Guard Boat Yard", June 15, 1917.

14. *Daily Star*, "College Point", September 5, 1917.

15. Military Service Record, New York State Archives.

16. *Daily Star*, "College Point Sends 250 Men to the Service", January 29, 1918.

Camp Upton and Beyond

1. Crawford, Gilbert H. *302nd Engineers: A History*, 1919.

2. Adler, Julius Ochs. *History of the 306th Infantry*, 1935.

3. *Daily Star*, "Drafted Man Writes of Camp Conditions", September 13, 1917.

4. *Flushing Daily Times*, "176th District Send 42 Men to Camp Upton", December 8, 1917.

5. *Flushing Daily Times*, "Activities of Red Cross in College Point", August 25, 1917.

6. Boughton, V.T. *History of the Eleventh Engineers*, J. J. Little and Ives Company: New York, 1927.

7. Tiebout, Frank Bosworth. *A History of the 305th Infantry*, 305th Auxiliary, New York. 1919.

From England to France

1. Crawford, Gilbert H., 302nd Engineers: A History, 1919.

2. *Chemical Warfare in World War One: The American Experience 1917-1918.*

3. *Daily Star*, "Be On Guard", December 12, 1917.

4. ibid. *Chemical Warfare in World War One.*

5. Heller, Charles E. *Chemical Warfare in World War One: The American Experience 1917-1918*. Leavenworth Papers: 1984.

6. ibid. *Chemical Warfare in World War One*

7. Zapotoczny, Walter S. *The Use of Poison Gas in World War I and the Effect on Society*: 2007.

8. Chemical Warfare and Medical Response During World War http://ajph. aphapublications.org/doi/abs/10.2105/AJPH.2007.111930

9. Weapons of War - Machine Gun http://www.firstworldwar.com/weaponry/machineguns.htm

10. Duffy, Ward E., Lieutenant, *The G. P. F. Book, Regimental History of the Three Hundred & Third Field Artillery*, 1921.

11. ibid. Jacobson, Gerald F. *History of the 107th Infantry, U.S.*

12. ibid.

13. Doughboy Center, Divisional Machinegun Units http://www.worldwar1.com/dbc/divmguns.htm

To Their Everlasting Credit George Andrew Rauh

1. *Daily Star*, "College Point Hero Made Good On His Promise", February 4, 1918.

2. Burial File, National Archives and Records Administration, College Park, MD.

3. American Battle Monuments Commission, http://www.abmc.gov/cemeteries/cemeteries.php

4. Military Service Record, New York State Archives.

5. ibid. "College Point Hero Made Good On His Promise"

6. ibid.

7. Beamish, Richard J, and March, Francis A., Ph.D., *America's Part in the World War*, The John C. Winston Company: 1919.

8. ibid. "College Point Hero Made Good On His Promise"

9. ibid. Burial File

10. ibid.

11. *Brooklyn Standard Union*, "Military Services For World War Dead", April 7, 1922.

Rudolph Brugger

1. World War One Draft Registration Card, 1917-1918, Ancestry.com

2. *Daily Star*, "Military Authorities Investigating Death of Rudolph Brugger", February 27, 1918.

3. Military Service Record, New York State Archives.

4. Divisional Officers Designated by the Division Commander, *Official History of the 82ⁿᵈ Division American Expeditionary Forces 1917-1919*. Bobbs-Merrill Company: Indianapolis, IN: 1919.

5. *Brooklyn Daily Eagle*, "L.I. Soldier Suicide At Atlanta Camp", February 27, 1918.

6. ibid. "Military Authorities Investigating Death of Rudolph Brugger"

7. *Daily Long Island Farmer*, "Suicide At Camp Gordon", February 27, 1918.

8. ibid. "L.I. Soldier Suicide At Atlanta Camp"

9. *Daily Star*, "College Point Soldier Dies At Camp Gordon", February 25, 1918.

10. *Daily Star*, Private Brugger Interred With Military Honors", March 18, 1918.

Oscar Ammann

1. *Brooklyn Daily Eagle*, "Two College Point Men Reported Dead", March 13, 1918.

2. *Daily Star*, "Lawrence Trimble Is Wounded In Action", September 2, 1918.

3. Military Service Records, New York State Archives.

4. *Brooklyn Daily Eagle*, "Lt. Baumert Not Killed as Reported", October 3, 1918.

5. Gilbert, Martin. *The First World Ward: A Complete History*, Henry Hold & Company: New York, 1994.

6. *Brooklyn Daily Eagle*, "Ammon Killed by Bullet", April 6, 1918.

7. *Daily Star* "Oscar Ammann of College Pt. Reported Killed in Action", March 12, 1918.

8. Burial File, National Archives and Records Administration, College Park, MD.

9. Email from Nathan Rouse, ed. Grandpa's World War I Diary http://e.wa/home.mindspring.com/wwdiary/

10. Ammon, Oscar, http://www.abmc.gov/search/wwi_state_list.php

11. Duffy, Francis P. *Father Duffy's Story: A Tale of Honor and Heroism, of Life and Death with the Fighting Sixty-Ninth*, George H. Doran Company: New York, 1919.

12. Harris, Stephen L. *Duffy's War*, Washington, DC: Potomac Books, 2006.

13. *Brooklyn Daily Eagle*, "$30,000 Endowment to College Pt. Inst.", May 8, 1918.

14. *Daily Star*, "College Point Pays Homage to Old Glory", June 17, 1918.

15. *Daily Star*, "Service Flag Honors Former Pupils Here", September 17, 1918.

16. *Daily Star*, "Emil Ammann to Visit Grave of War Hero Son", June 14, 1921.

17. *Daily Star*, "Mrs. Ammann Given a Traveling Bag", May 19, 1930.

18. ibid. *Father Duffy's Story*

19. *Brooklyn Daily Eagle*, "City Unveils Heroic Statue to Fr. Duffy", May 3, 1937.

William Emil Buerger

1. Military Service Record, New York State Archives.

2. *Daily Star*, "Graduation Exercises", June 20, 1911.

3. *Brooklyn Daily Eagle*, "Emil Buerger", June 7, 1911.

4. ibid. Military Service Record

5. Burial Record, National Archives and Records Administration, College Park, MD.

6. ibid. Military Service Record

7. *Newtown Register*, "Recent Weddings", January 25, 1917.

8. ibid. Burial Record

9. *USS Burrows*, http://www.history.navy.mil/photos/sh-usn/usnsh-b/dd29.htm

10. ibid. Burial Record

11. ibid.

12. *Brooklyn Daily Eagle*, "His Thanks Come After Death Note", March 27, 1918.

13. Military Service Record, New York State Archives.

14. ibid. Burial Record

15. ibid.

16. ibid.

Charles O. Mahler

1. *Flushing Daily Times*, "College Point Youth Dies At Camp Upton", March 15, 1918.

2. Military Service Record, New York State Archives.

3. United States World War One Draft Registration Card, 1917-1918, Ancestry.com.

4. *Daily Star*, "College Point Soldier Dies At Camp Upton", March 15, 1918.

5. *Daily Star*, "Funeral Of A Soldier", March 19, 1918.

6. ibid. Military Service Record

7. Mahler Family Census Records, 1840-1880, Ancestry.com.

8. *Daily Star*, "Thirty-Eight Stars In Flag", March 19, 1918.

9. ibid. Military Service Records

I Long To Go Home

1. *Brooklyn Daily Eagle*, "College Point Is Busy Place: Teems With War Industry", April 28, 1918.

2. *Brooklyn Daily Eagle*, "Set Up Private War Zone; Barred Teuton; Fined $10", May 25, 1917.

3. *Brooklyn Daily Eagle*, "500 Aliens Become Citizens At Upton" , May 22, 1918.

4. *Newtown Register*, "German Language Press Hit Hard", May 30, 1918.

5. *Flushing Daily Times*, "College Point Soldier Gassed By The Germans", June 13, 1918.

6. *Daily Star*, "Red Cross Receipts Will Be More Than $15,000", May 29, 1918.

7. *Brooklyn Daily Eagle*, "A College Point Social Club", February 9, 1889.

8. *Brooklyn Daily Eagle*, "K. Of C. Campaign Is Extended A Week", December 17, 1917.

9. *New York Tribune*, "News In Brief", February 11, 1918.

Thomas Henry Fagan

1. *Daily Star*, "College Point", July 17, 1917.

2. *Daily Star*, "College Point Man Killed In France", June 21, 1918.

3. Eck, Robert J., *"Tommy, We'll Miss You Son"* Unpublished Manuscript. Unless otherwise noted, much of Thomas' time in England is excerpted from this manuscript, with the permission of the author's family.

4. *Daily Star*, "Handiwork Exhibited", May 10, 1915.

5. *Daily Star*, "College Point", December 26, 1917.

Alfred Stengel

1. *307ᵗʰ Infantry Memorial in Central Park*, http://www.77thinfdivroa.org/news/news_NYCmem.htm

2. *Flushing Daily Times*, "College Point Youth Held As a Deserter", November 24, 1917.

3. Military Service Record, New York State Archives.

4. United States World War One Draft Registration Card, 1917-1918, Ancestry.com.

5. Military Service Record, New York State Archives.

6. *Daily Star*, "Friends Pay Honor To Drafted Men", September 20, 1917.

7. ibid. Military Service Record

8. *Daily Star*, "Gives 2 Sons to Army; Has Done Much Knitting", February 28, 1918.

9. *Daily Star*, "College Pt. Knitting Club Has Aided 159 In Service", January 31, 1918.

10. ibid. "Gives 2 Sons to Army; Has Done Much Knitting"

11. *Through the War with Company D 307ᵗʰ Infantry 77ᵗʰ Division*, New York, 1919.

12. Sergeant Grosjean, Jean Company "F" 307ᵗʰ Infantry Regiment 77ᵗʰ Division. Transcribed by Mr. Robert von Pentz: http://www.longwood.k12.ny.us/history/upton.grossjean.htm

13. ibid. *Through the War with Company D 307ᵗʰ Infantry 77ᵗʰ Division*

14. *Flushing Daily Times*, "Flushing and College Point Men Killed in Action", July 22, 1918.

15. *Brooklyn Daily Eagle*, "Edward L. Martin", December 24, 1918.

16. Burial Record, National Archives and Records Administration, College Park, MD.

17. *Daily Star,* "Service Flag Has 54 Stars", July 17, 1918.

18. *History of the 77th Division,* http://www.longwood.k12.ny.us/history/upton/phase4.htm

19. *The Legends of "Kilroy Was Here",* http://www.kilroywashere.org/001-Pages/01-0KilroyLegends.html

20. U.S. Army Transport Service, Passenger Lists 1910-1939, Ancestry.com

21. *Daily Star,* "Body of War Hero is Brought Back Home", June 4, 1921.

22. ibid.

23. *Flushing Daily Times,* "Flushing and College Point Men Killed in Action", July 22, 1918.

24. *Brooklyn Daily Eagle,* "Pvt. Edward L. Martin", December 24, 1918.

25. *North Shore Daily Journal,* "500 Attend Services for Edward Martin", February 14, 1938.

July - September

1. *New York Herald,* "Central Powers Cracking", September 16, 1918.

2. *Flushing Daily Times,* "Says Candy She Ate Held Glass", July 13, 1918.

3. *Brooklyn Daily Eagle,* "In German Circles", June 16, 1915.

4. *Daily Star,* "Finds Selling Daschunds Trading With the Enemy", September 17, 1918.

5. *Anti-German Hysteria During World War One,* http://www.johnheinl.net/LHserver/JP-german61001.htm

6. *Flushing Daily Times,* "176th Sends 72 Men to Camp Upton", July 26, 1918.

7. *Flushing Daily Times,* "176th Board to Send 18 Men to Camp Gordon", August 17, 1918.

8. *Brooklyn Daily Eagle,* "Sent To Camp Gordon, Ga., August 23", September 1, 1918.

9. *Brooklyn Daily Eagle,* "Lt. Baumert Not Killed as Reported", October 3, 1918

10. *The Sun,* "Married Before Sailing", November 5, 1918.

John Harold Embree

1. Military Service Record, New York State Archives.

2. *Daily Long Island Farmer*, "Sergeant Harold Embree Killed", December 24, 1918.

3. *Second Battle of the Marne*, http://www.worldwar1.com/dbc/2marne.htm

4. Duffy, Francis E. *Father Duffy's Story*. George H. Doran Company: 1919.

5. The author is indebted to descendants of J. Newlin Embree for permitting access to the very large collection of letters saved by John G. Embree.

6. Tom Sharkey, http://en.wikipedia.org/wiki/Tom_Sharkey

7. Burial File, National Archives and Records Administration, College Park, MD.

8. ibid. Letters of John G. Embree

9. ibid.

10. ibid. Burial File

11. *Brooklyn Daily Eagle*, "Vassar Girls At Home", December 1, 1917.

12. ibid. Letters of John G. Embree

13. *The Courier, Brookfield, New York*, "Miss Cynthia York Married", August 1, 1928.

14. ibid. Letters of John G. Embree

15. *Daily Star*, "Body of Sergt. Embree Back In College Point", August 4, 1921.

16. *Brooklyn Daily Eagle*, "To Graduate 76 At Flushing H.S.", June 27, 1921.

17. *Brooklyn Daily Eagle*, "John G. Embree, 49, Dies in Hospital", June 28, 1921.

18. *Daily Star*, "All College Point Pays Homage To John G. Embree", June 30, 1921.

19. *Cornell Daily Sun*, "Service Held in Commemoration of Cornellians", June 9, 1919.

August Bigler

1. *Daily Star*, "42 for Upton from Dist. 176", December 5, 1917.

2. Military Service Record, New York State Archives.

3. *Flushing Daily Times*, "Gus Bigler Falls in Action Against Huns", September 14, 1918.

4. *Daily Star*, "Chaplain Pays Tribute to Bigler, Killed in France", October 3, 1918.

5. U.S. Army Transport Service, Passenger Lists 1910-1939, Ancestry.com.

6. Burial File, National Archives and Records Administration, College Park, MD.

7. *Brooklyn Daily Eagle*, "Funeral Services for Bigler", July 13, 1921.

8. *Flushing Daily Times*, "Jacob Bigler Reported Missing; May be Dead", December 2, 1918.

9. *Daily Star*, Body of War Hero is Brought Home", July 12, 1921

10. ibid. Military Service Record

The Lord Was With Me

1. *Flushing Daily Times*, "College Point Dance Hall As War Factory", October 4, 1918.

2. *Daily Star*, "Queens Borough Becoming A Ship Building Center", October 5, 1918.

3. *Flushing Daily Times*, "College Point Plans Carnival and Block Party", September 9, 1918.

4. *Flushing Daily Times*, "Block Party Earned $3,551", November 7, 1918..

5. *Daily Star*, Name Chiefs for War Loan Drive in College Point", September 3, 1918.

6. *Memorial Day Exercises Program*, Oscar Amman Post 853: May 31, 1920.

7. *Brooklyn Daily Eagle*, "Carry Uncle Sam in Flushing Street", April 15, 1918

8. *Flushing Daily Times*, "College Pointer's Pal Killed at His Side", September 13, 1918.

9. *Flushing Daily Times*, "Eager to Fight, He is Rejected at Camp", September 13, 1918.

10. *Flushing Daily Times*, "Eagle Pass Tex., Another "No Man's Land", September 19, 1918.

11. *Daily Star*, "First Class Private Martin Zwicke", November 14, 1918

12. *Daily Star*, "Private Emil Schnell", November 29, 1918.

13. *Flushing Daily Times*, "Pvt. Gray of College Point Is Wounded", October 4, 1918.

14. *Daily Star*, "College Point", December 5, 1918.

15. *Baltimore Sun*, "To Aid War Crippled", August 4, 1918.

16. *St. Mihiel: A Push Forward*, http://www.firstdivisionmuseum.org/museum/online/toward_the_front/st_mihiel/default.aspx

17. Crawford, Gilbert H., *302ⁿᵈ Engineers: A History*, 1919.

18. *Meuse River – Argonne Forest Offensive*, http://www.historyofwar.org/articles/battles_meuse_argonne.html

19. Tiebout, Frank Bosworth. *A History of the 305ᵗʰ Infantry*, 305ᵗʰ Auxiliary: New York, 1919.

20. Glock, Carl Edward, *History of the 316ᵗʰ Infantry Regiment in the World War 1918*.

21. O'Shea, Stephen, *Back to the Front*, Avon Books: New York, NY 1996.

22. ibid. *History of the 316ᵗʰ Infantry Regiment in the World War 1918*.

James Joseph Powers

1. Hendricks, Charles. *Combat and Construction: U.S. Army Engineers in World War I.*

2. Baptism Record from Church of the Assumption, Peekskill, NY.

3. Ship Manifest, *SS St. Paul*, New York, June 23, 1900, Ancestry.co.

4. Military Service Record, New York State Archives.

5. Boughton, V.T. *History of the Eleventh Engineers* J. J. Little and Ives Company, New York 1927.

6. ibid.

7. ibid.

8. ibid.

9. Burial File, National Archives and Records Administration, College Park, MD.

10. *Brooklyn Daily Eagle*, " Sergeant James J. Powers", November 26, 1918.

11. ibid. Burial File.

12. ibid.

Emil John Schwab

1. Military Service Record, New York State Archives.

2. Glock, Carl Edward, *History of the 316th Infantry Regiment in the World War 1918*, Pittsburg, 1919.

3. *SS Kaiser Wilhelm II*, http://en.wikipedia.org/wiki/SS_Kaiser_Wilhelm_II

4. ibid. *History of the 316th Infantry Regiment in the World War 1918*.

5. ibid.

6. ibid.

7. U.S. Army Transport Service, Passenger Lists 1910-1939, Ancestry.com.

8. *Daily Star*, "College Point", June 9, 1922.

9. Burial File, National Archives and Records Administration, College Park, MD.

Arthur Bartholomew Rooney

1. Military Service Cards, New York State Archives.

2. Glock, Carl Edward, *History of the 316th Infantry Regiment in the World War 1918*.

3. Burial File, National Archives and Records Administration, College Park, MD.

4. U. S. Army Transport Service, Passenger Lists 1910-1939, Ancestry.com.

5. *Brooklyn Daily Eagle*, "To Bury Queens Soldier", August 11, 1921.

6. *Daily Star*, "Body of Arthur Rooney Back In College Point", August 11, 1921.

7. *Brooklyn Daily Eagle*, "Charles Ruckdaschel", November 20, 1918.

8. ibid. Military Service Record

Christian Geidel

1. *Brooklyn Daily Eagle*, "Christian Geidel", March 13, 1940.

2. *Daily Star*, "Chris Geidel, College Pointer", March 19, 1927.

3. United States World War One Draft Registration Card, 1917-1918, Ancestry.com.

4. *Daily Star*, "Friends Pay Honor To Drafted Men", September 22, 1917.

5. Military Service Cards, New York State Archives.

6. Tiebout, Frank Bosworth. *A History of the 305ᵗʰ Infantry*, 305ᵗʰ Auxiliary, New York. 1919.

7. ibid.

8. Adler, Julius Ochs. *History of the 306ᵗʰ Infantry*, 1935.

9. Burial File, National Archives and Records Administration, College Park, MD.

10. *New York Times,* "4 Veterans Get Medals", June 7, 1933.

11. *New York Evening Telegram*, "New York Acclaims Own Heroes of the 77ᵗʰ Division", May 6, 1919.

12. *Flushing Daily Times*, "Chris. Geidell Killed in Battle", October 18, 1918.

13. ibid. Burial File

14. *New York Times.* "Sweaters, Perhaps Raincoats, Advised for Today's Game", October 12, 1921.

15. Covil, Eric C. "Radio and its Impact on the Sports World", *American Sportscasters Online.*

16. *Daily Star,* "College Point War Hero Laid To Rest", October 14, 1921.

17. *Daily Star*, "Fred Geidel", December 17, 1919.

Louis Bismarck Doerr

1. Letter to author from Carol Johnert, wife of Doerr family descendant Roy Johnert.

2. *Brooklyn Daily Eagle*, "Eagle Baseball Trophy for Public School No. 27", June 28, 1906.

3. United States World War One Draft Registration Card, 1917-1918, Ancestry.com.

4. Military Service Record, New York State Archives.

5. *Daily Star*, "College Point", February 9, 1918.

6. Crawford, Gilbert H., *302ⁿᵈ Engineers: A History*, 1919.

7. ibid.

8. *Flushing Daily Times*, "Writes How Air-Raid Stopped Baseball Game", August 14, 1918.

9. ibid. *302nd Engineers: A History.*

10. ibid.

11. ibid. Divisional Citation: Captain Robert C. O'Donnell, Headquarters Company, 302nd Engineers.

12. *Flushing Daily Times*, "Writes That Louis Doerr Has Fallen", October 21, 1918.

13. *Daily Star*, "Body of Sergeant Louis Doerr To Be Buried Saturday", September 1, 1921.

14. ibid.

15. ibid. "Eagle Baseball Trophy for Public School No. 27."

16. U.S. Army Transport Service, Passenger Lists 1910-1939, Ancestry.com.

17. *Daily Star*, "College Pt. Pays Last Tribute To Hero Of Argonne", September 6, 1921.

18. *Daily Star*, "College Point", September 3, 1921.

19. ibid. "Body of Sergeant Louis Doerr To Be Buried Saturday."

20. ibid. Military Service Record

21. ibid. "College Pt. Pays Last Tribute To Hero Of Argonne."

22. ibid. Carol Johnert to author.

23. *Daily Star*. "J. H. Gerlach Dies; Loose-Leaf Pioneer", September 1, 1921.

24. *Daily Star*, "William Kaufman", August 22, 1923.

Ernest B. Plitt

1. *New York Times*, "Touchard Retains Felipe Tennis Cup", June 5, 1910.

2. *New York Times*, "Plitt Wins Tennis Title", September 15, 1924.

3. *New York Times*, "Baker Beats Plitt", September 20, 1926.

4. *Daily Star*, "Embree Tennis Champion", September 13, 1915.

5. *Daily Standard Union*, "Class of 1904", July 5, 1908.

6. United State World War One Draft Registration Card, 1917-1918, Ancestry.com.

7. Military Service Record, New York State Archives.

8. *Suffolk County News*, "Among the Strangest Documents", April 5, 1935. Submitted as proof of his last will and testament to settle his mother's estate upon her death in 1935. Letter held in estate documents in the Brooklyn, NY Surrogates Court.

9. ibid. Military Service Record

10. *Syracuse Post-Standard*, "Private Ching Kee", September 3, 1918.

11. Silverstar 10 General Orders: GHQ, American Expeditionary Forces, Citation Orders No. 5, June 3, 1919.

12. ibid. Military Service Record

13. *Utica Herald-Dispatch*, "Harold Bennison", November 12, 1918.

14. Malsbury, George E. Dr., Editor, *Southern California Practitioner*, Volume 34.

15. *A Typical Hospital Center*, U.S. Army Medical Department, http://history.amedd.army.mil/booksdocs/wwi/adminamerexp/chapter22.html

16. Burial Record, National Archives and Records Administration, College Park, MD.

17. ibid. *A Typical Hospital Center.*

18. *Brooklyn Daily Eagle*, "Pvt. Ernest Plitt", October 21, 1918.

19. Williams, Paul Benjamin. *United States Lawn Tennis Association and the World War,* Robert Hamilton Co.: New York, 1921.

20. U.S. Army Transport Service, Passenger Lists 1910-1939, Ancestry.com.

21. *Daily Star*, "Elmhurst Post Men Escort Hero's Body", February 14, 1921.

22. ibid. U.S. Army Transport Service, Passenger Lists

23. ibid. "Among the Strangest Documents"

Stephen Melbourne Schwab

1. Schlegel, Carl Wilhelm. *German-American Families in the United States, Volume I*, The American Historical Society: New York, 1916.

2. Haas, James E., *Conrad Poppenhusen: The Life of a German-American Industrial Pioneer*, Gateway Press: Baltimore, MD 2004.

3. ibid. *German-American Families in the United State, Volume I.*

4. *Brooklyn Daily Eagle*, "Found Missing Wife and Sons", January 30, 1903.

5. ibid. "Found Missing Wife and Sons"

6. *Daily Star*, "Interesting News From College Point", February 10, 1905.

7. *Brooklyn Daily Eagle*, "Queens School Games", May 14, 1905.

8. *Brooklyn Daily Eagle*, "Lt. Stephen Schwab Killed", November 14, 1918.

9. Jacobson, Gerald F. *History of the 107th Infantry*. Seventh Regiment Armory, New York City, 1920.

10. *Daily Star*, "Sailed On the Red Cross", September 8, 1914

11. ibid. *History of the 107th Infantry*.

12. Krayer, Nicholas H., *History of Company "E", 107th Infantry*.

13. *Schenectady Gazette*, "Second Infantry Officer Hurt", October 2, 1917.

14. ibid. *History of Company "E", 107th Infantry*

15. *Flushing Daily Times*, "Larry Trimble of College Point Badly Wounded", September 4, 1918.

16. Military Service Record, New York State Archives.

17. ibid. *History of Company "E", 107th Infantry*

18. ibid.

19. ibid.

20. ibid. *History of the 107th Infantry*

21. ibid. "Lt. Stephen Schwab Killed"

22. Military Service Record, New York State Archives.

23. ibid. Burial Record.

24. ibid.

Edward J. Stack

1. *Daily Star*, "Eleventh Street Outing", August 21, 1914.

2. *Brooklyn Daily Eagle*, "Brooklyn Soldiers in Wadsworth Play", March 7, 1918.

3. Haas, James E. *Conrad Poppenhusen: The Life of a German-American Industrial Pioneer*, Gateway Press, Baltimore, MD, 2004.

4. Harris, Stephen L. *Duty, Honor, Privilege: New York's Silk Stocking Regiment and the Breaking of the Hindenburg Line*. Brassey's Inc. Washington, DC, 2001.

5. ibid.

6. ibid.

7. Military Service Record, New York State Archives.

8. *Brooklyn Daily Eagle*, "Shoots Wounded German to End His Suffering", December 6, 1918.

9. Jacobson, Gerald F. *History of the 107th Infantry, U.S.A.*

10. New York State Military Museum, *107th Infantry Regiment World War One* http://dmna.state.ny.us/historic/reghist/wwi/infantry/107thInf/107thInfMain.htm

11. ibid. *History of the 107th Infantry, U.S.A.*

12. *Daily Star*, "Body of Edward Stack Is Returned From France", April 9, 1921.

13. *Brooklyn Daily Eagle*, "Brooklyn Troops Home With the 107th", March 10, 1919.

14. O'Ryan, Maj. Gen. John F. *The Story of the 27th Division*, 2 vols. New York,: Wynkoop, Hallenbeck, Crawford, 1921.

15. ibid. Military Service Record

Hyman Lashiwer

1. *Brooklyn Daily Eagle*, "Lt. Thomas J. Taylor Gets Distinguished Service Cross", February 7, 1919.

2. Military Service Record, New York State Archives.

3. U.S. Army Transport Service, Passenger Lists 1910-1939, Ancestry.com.

4. ibid. Military Service Record

5. *Daily Star*, "Becker Missing In Action", August 4, 1918.

6. ibid. Military Service Record.

7. Burial Record, National Archives and Records Administration, College Park, MD.

8. ibid.

9. ibid.

10. U.S. Army Transport Service, Passenger Lists 1910-1939, Ancestry.com.

11. *Daily Star*, Military Funeral For College Pointer Killed in Battle", February 23, 1922.

12. ibid. "Lt. Thomas J. Taylor Gets Distinguished Service Cross."

13. Death Certificate, Eva Kessler, Connecticut State Archives, Hartford, CT.

14. Email from Lisa Vaeth, Jewish Federation of Greater Hartford, December 14, 2009.

Louis George Fritz

1. Haas, James E., *This Gunner At His Piece: College Point, New York & the Civil War*: Gateway Press: Baltimore, MD, 2002.

2. *Brooklyn Daily Eagle*, "Five Brooklyn Sailors Accepted for Merchant Marines", August 25, 1918.

3. *Army Transport Meade Becomes Training Ship for Merchant Marine Apprentices*, "International Marine Engineering, Volume XXIII, January to December 1918: New York, Aldrich Publishing Company, 1918.

4. *How Young Americans Are Taught to Man Our New Merchant Marine, 1918.* Emergency Fleet News, U.S. Shipping Board Emergency Fleet Corporation Philadelphia May 20, 1918.

5. ibid

6. "Stricken With Appendicitis", *Daily Star*, October 5, 1918.

7. "Dies Month After Joining The Merchant Marine", *Daily Star*, October 7, 1918.

8. "Sailors Escort Body of Louis Fritz To Grace", *Daily Star*, October 10, 1918.

Benjamin Franklin Blue

1. *Brooklyn Daily Eagle*, "A "Blue" Challenge", August 26, 1902.

2. Returns from Regular Army Infantry Regiments, 1821-1916, Ancestry. com

3. https://www.hmdb.org/marker.asp?marker=2993 Submitted on October 15, 2007, by Craig Swain of Leesburg, Virginia.

4. *Daily Star*, "Death of Sergeant B. Blue", March 11, 1912.

5. *Daily Star*, "A Military Funeral", March 13, 1912.

6. *Brooklyn Daily Eagle*, October 11, 1899.

7. *Philadelphia Inquirer*, "Sergeant Blue Removed From Schriver's Home", January 8, 1912.

8. *Brooklyn Daily Eagle*, "Long Island Personals", October 11, 1899.

9. *Brooklyn Daily Eagle*, "A Chip Off The Old Block", October 5, 1900.

10. http://www.hmdb.org/marker.asp?marker=2993 Submitted on October 15, 2007, by Craig Swain of Leesburg, Virginia.

11. *Daily Star*, "Bugler's Life No Song, He Writes", June 7, 1918.

12. ibid.

13. http://ibiblio.org/hyperwar/AMH/XX/WWI/Army/Medical/IX/ USA-Med-IX-2.html *The Medical Department of the United States Army in the World War Vol. IX*: Communicable and other Diseases.

14. Burial Record, National Archives and Records Administration, College Park, MD

15. *Daily Star*, "Body Of Bugler Blue Brought From France", May 24, 1921.

Louis Schmidt

1. *Daily Star*, "Military Honors For Louis Schmidt", October 14, 1918.

2. *Daily Star*, "Drafted Two Weeks Ago, Dies Of Influenza", October 14, 1918.

3. *New York Times*, "Influenza Epidemic Hits Camp Devens", September 15, 1918.

4. Crosby, Alfred W. *America's Forgotten Pandemic: The Influenza of 1918*, Cambridge University Press, 1989.

5. *New York Times*, "To Fight Spanish Grip", September 16, 1918.

6. *New York Times*, "More Influenza Found", September 17, 1918.

7. *New York Times*, "Think Influenza Came in U-Boat", September 19, 1918.

8. *New York Times*, "How to Avoid All Respiratory Diseases", September 22, 1918.

9. *New York Times*, "The Influenza", October 3, 1918.

10. *Daily Star*, "Mrs. Mottram Dies, Victim Of Influenza", October 28, 1918.

11. *Daily Star*, "Joseph Schmidt", October 31, 1918.

12. *New York Times*, "Influenza Cases Drop 305 in City", October 21, 1918.

13. *New York Times*, "Cases Drop in Army Camps", October 22, 1918.

14. *New York Times*, "Vaccine a Success at Camp Dix", October 23, 1918.

15. *New York Times*, "Beware of Sure Cures", October 27, 1918.

16. *Brooklyn Daily Eagle*, "Open Nostrils! End a Cold or Influenza", November 12, 1918.

17. *Watertown Daily Times*, "Druggist Still Asked to Conserve Stocks of Vaporub Needed in Flu Districts", November 14, 1918.

18. *Brooklyn Daily Eagle*, "Open Nostrils! End a Cold or Influenza", November 12, 1918.

19. *The Influenza Pandemic of 1918*, http://virus.stanford.edu/uda/

20. *New York Times*, "Influenza Still Spreads in City", September 26, 1918.

21. *Flushing Daily Times*, "Funeral Services for Louis Schmidt", October 11, 1918.

22. *Daily Star*, "Military Honors For Louis Schmidt", October 14, 1918.

August William Breisacher

1. *Brooklyn Daily Eagle*, "To Honor Fallen Heroes", August 31, 1921.

2. United States World War One Draft Registration Card, 1917-1918, Ancestry.com.

3. Military Service Record, New York State Archives.

4. Cutchins, John A. *History of the Twenty-Ninth Division: Blue and Gray 1919*. Philadelphia: 1921.

5. *Chemical Warfare in World War One: The American Experience 1917-1918*.

6. Cochrane, Rexmond C. *Gas Warfare in World War I*: U.S. Army Chemical Corps Historical Studies: October, 1959.

7. ibid. Military Service Record.

8. *Brooklyn Daily Eagle*, "Pvt. Walter J. J. Garvin", December 6, 1918.

9. Ewing, Joseph H., *29th Infantry Division: A Short History of a Fighting Division*, Turner Publishing Company: Paducah, KY 1992.

10. ibid. Military Service Record

11. ibid. *History of the Twenty-Ninth Division: Blue and Gray 1919.*

12. ibid. Military Service Record

13. *Brooklyn Daily Eagle*, "Pvt. Walter J. J. Garvin", December 24, 1918.

14. Burial File, National Archives and Records Administration, College Park, MD.

15. ibid.

16. *Brooklyn Daily Eagle*, "Brooklyn Artillerymen of 27th Division", March 13, 1919.

17. U.S. Army Transport Service, Passenger Lists 1910-1939, Ancestry.com.

18. ibid. Burial File

19. ibid "To Honor Fallen Heroes"

20. *Brooklyn Daily Eagle,* "Pvt. August Breisacher", November 30, 1918.

21. *Daily Star*, "His Comrades Honor College Point Hero", September 2, 1921.

John Baptist Endres

1. Military Service Record, New York State Archives.

2. World War I Draft Registration Card, 1917-1918, Ancestry.com.

3. Email to author from John B. Endres' great nephew, John Schmermund, July 12, 2010.

4. *Daily Star*, "College Points Claim Championship", December 8, 1915.

5. *Daily Star*, "College Point Club And Elms Play Tie Game", December 4, 1916.

6. ibid. World War I Draft Registration Card, 1917-1918.

7. Military Service Record, New York State Archives.

8. Baker, Leslie S., *The Story of Company B 106th Machine Gun Battalion 27th Division, U.S.A.* 1920.

9. ibid.

10. Schuyler, Philip, V.R. Sergeant, *"C" Company 106th Machine Gun Battalion 27th Division, U.S.A.* Patterson Press, New York: 1919.

11. ibid.

12. ibid. *The Story of Company B.*

13. Burial File, National Archives and Records Administration, College Park, MD.

14. ibid. Military Service Record

15. ibid.

16. *Daily Star*, "College Point", December 31, 1918.

17. *Daily Star*, "Post To Pay Respects to Endres' Memory", April 8, 1921.

18. *Brooklyn Daily Eagle*, "Funeral of J. B. Endres, Soldier-Policeman", April 14, 1921.

19. *New York Times*, "Police Pay Tribute to Their War Dead", June 21, 1923.

20. ibid. Military Service Record

Thomas Joseph McCormick

1. World War One Draft Registration Card, 1917-1918, Ancestry.com.

2. Email from John McCormick's Grandson, also named John McCormick.

3. Military Service Record, New York State Archives.

4. Beamish, Richard J. and March, Francis A. Ph.D. *America's Part in the World War.* The John C. Winston Company: Philadelphia, PA. 1919.

5. ibid.

6. Duffy, Ward E., Lieutenant, *The G. P. F. Book, Regimental History of the Three Hundred & Third Field Artillery*, 1921.

7. Military Service Record, New York State Archives.

8. *1ˢᵗ Battalion, 26ᵗʰ Infantry Regiment: "Blue Spaders"* http://www.globalsecurity.org/military/agency/army/1-26inf.htm

9. *Yanks In France:* http://homepage.mac.com/oldtownman/ww1/yanks.html

10. Letters from John McCormick, Thomas McCormick's nephew born in 1929.

11. *Brooklyn Daily Eagle*, "Pvt. Thomas P. McCormick", November 29, 1918.

12. *A History of University of California at San Francisco* http://history.library.ucsf.edu/1899_affiliated_colleges.html

13. Burial File, National Archives and Records Administration, College Park, MD.

14. ibid. *The G.P.F. Book*.

15. ibid. Burial File

16. ibid.

17. ibid.

18. U.S. Army Transport Service, Passenger Lists, 1910-1939, Ancestry.com

19. *Daily Star*, "Body Of Another War Hero Comes Home", June 8, 1921.

20. ibid. Email from John McCormick's grandson.

21. ibid.

22. *Daily Star*, "Private Thomas B. McCormick", November 27, 1918.

Albert W. Frey

1. *Brooklyn Daily Eagle*, "Three Boys Burned", November 8, 1896.

2. *Daily Star*, "Poppenhusen Institute", March 8, 1911.

3. *Daily Star*, "Edward A. Frey", June 11, 1917.

4. *Daily Star*, "Transfers Management", January 22, 1917.

5. *Daily Star*, "Farewell Honors For Drafted Men", October 11, 1917.

6. *Brooklyn Daily Eagle*, "Opportunities For Hustling Printer", October 21, 1917.

7. Military Service Record, New York State Archives.

8. *Daily Star*, "Is Made Sergeant", February 2, 1918.

9. *Daily Star*, "College Point", March 16, 1918.

10. Historical Impressions Page, http://www.327gir.com/wwone327.html

11. Ferrel, Robert H., *The Question of MacArthur's Reputation: Cote de Chaillon, October 14-16, 1918*. University of Missouri Press: Columbia, MO, 2008.

12. Divisional Officers Designated by the Division Commander, *Official History of the 82nd Division American Expeditionary Forces 1917-1919*, Bobbs-Merrill Company: Indianapolis, IN, 1919.

13. *Daily Star*, "Private Albert W. Frey", November 29, 1918.

14. Burial File, National Archives and Records Administration, College Park, MD.

15. ibid.

16. U.S. Army Transport Service, Passenger Lists, 1910-1939, Ancestry.com

17. ibid. Burial File

18. *Daily Star*, "College Point", August 31, 1921.

19. ibid. Burial File

20. *Brooklyn Daily Eagle*, Anna W. Frey", March 14, 1935.

21. *Brooklyn Daily Eagle*, "Boy's Hand Crushed", March 28, 1901.

22. The Museum of Printing, http://www.museumofprinting.org/Library.html

William John Nicholas Mohrmann

1. U. S. Navy Death Record, Ancestry.com.

2. World War One Draft Registration Card, 1917-1918, Ancestry.com.

3. Military Service Record, New York State Archives.

4. *The Pelham Bay Naval Reserve Training Station*, "The Architectural Forum", July 1918.

5. *Brooklyn Daily Eagle*, "One Woman Among Ten Thousand Men", September 14, 1918.

6. ibid.

7. *Epidemics of Influenza in the Navy During the Autumn of 1918*, Annual Report of the Secretary of the Navy, 1919.

8. ibid.

9. "The Story of Influenza", https://www.ncbi.nlm.nih.gov/books/NBK22148/

10. *Daily Star*, William J. M. Mohrmann", November 11, 1918.

11. *Long Island Daily Press*, "Marshal's Aide Drops Dead In Memorial Day Parade", May 31, 1940.

12. *Long Island Star Journal*, "Mrs. Mohrmann Memorialized", December 28, 1953.

Henry Zimmer

1. *The Traveler*, Southold, NY, August 4, 1893.

2. *Brooklyn Daily Eagle*, "Clara H. Zimmer", May 1, 1900.

3. ibid.

4. *Daily Star*, "College Point", February 7, 1910.

5. Military Service Record, New York State Archives.

6. U.S. Army Transport Service, Passenger Lists, 1910-1939, Ancestry.com

7. Ancestry.com.

8. Burial File, National Archives and Records Administration, College Park, MD.

9. River, T.M., M.D., *The American Journal of Public Health: Influenzal Meningitis*, 1922.

10. Brundage, John F. Historical Review: *Interactions between Influenza and Bacterial Respiratory Pathogens: Implications for Pandemic Preparedness.* https://www.ncbi.nlm.nih.gov/pubmed/16631551

11. ibid. Burial File

Arthur Kraemer

1. World War I Draft Registration Card, 1917-1918, Ancestry.com.

2. Military Service Record, New York State Archives.

3. *The World*, "Boys Wished To See Real Train Wreck", March 10, 1906.

4. *Daily Star*, "Three Young Train Wreckers Caught", March 10. 1906.

5. U.S. Army Transport Service, Passenger Lists 1910-1939, Ancestry.com.

6. ibid. Military Service Record.

7. Burial File, National Archives and Records Administration, College Park, MD.

8. Hungerford, Edward, *With the Doughboy in France: A Few Chapters of An American Effort.* The Macmillan Company: New York, 1920.

9. ibid. Burial File

10. ibid.

11. ibid.

12. ibid.

13. *Daily Star*, "College Point Soldier's Body From France", September 18, 1920.

14. *Brooklyn Standard Union*, "Jennie C. Kraemer", March 31, 1923.

15. *Daily Star*, "Otto Kraemer", June 2, 1925.

16. *Daily Star*, "No Slackers, Says Hook, On An Ammunition Train", November 18, 1918.

To Honor Fallen Heroes

1. *Daily Star*", "College Point Went Wild Over Peace Report", November 9, 1918.

2. *Daily Star*, "Day of Rejoicing in College Point", November 12, 1918

3. *Flushing Daily Times*, "50 Men Leave For Fort Totten", November 11, 1918.

4. ibid. "Day of Rejoicing in College Point"

5. *Flushing Daily Times*, "Town Goes Wild Again at News of Armistice", November 11, 1918.

6. *Flushing Daily Times*, "All the Libraries in Queens", November 13, 1918.

7. *Daily Star*, "College Point Unfurls A Flag With 600 Stars", November 25, 1918.

8. ibid.

9. *Daily Star*, "572 College Point Men In U. S. Service", September 6, 1918.

10. *Daily Star*, "Will Beautify Station Entrance", April 14, 1917.

11. *Daily Star*, "2,000 Parade To Mark Fourth At College Point", July 5, 1917

12. *Daily Long Island Farmer*, "College Point's War Memorial", February 6, 1919.

13. *Brooklyn Daily Eagle*, "College Point Has Memorial", February 25, 1919.

14. Military Service Record, New York State Archives.

15. *Daily Sun*, "Mass Meeting For Memorial Tonight", November 19, 1919.

16. *Daily Star*, "Memorial Committee Welcomes Suggestions", December 15, 1919.

17. ibid.

18. *Daily Star*, "College Point To Give Prizes For Memorial Ideas", December 9, 1919.

19. *Daily Star*, "Committee Gives Memorial Prizes", February 10, 1920.

20. *Daily Star*, "Mr. and Mrs. Herman A. MacNeil", January 5, 1920.

21. *Daily Star*, "Flushing Unveils Monument", June 1, 1925.

22. *Daily Star*, "College Point to Have Parade and Program in Memorial Square", May 29, 1926.

23. *Brooklyn Daily Eagle*, "Four Memorials To Be Dedicated", May 19, 1930.

24. *Brooklyn Daily Eagle*, "Dedicate Monuments", May 30, 1930.

25. *Brooklyn Daily Eagle*, "Hero's Mother Unveils Plaque, May 31, 1930.

Epilogue

1. *Memorial Day Program Book, Oscar Ammann Post 853*, May 31, 1920.

2. ibid.

3. *Brooklyn Daily Eagle*, "Trade Depression Hits L.I. Aircraft Plant; Must Sell", April 8, 1924.

4. *Daily Star*, "College Point", April 17, 1924.

5. *Daily* Star, "Aero Industry Revival Seen In College Point", November 23, 1926.

6. *Daily Star*, "Sikorsky Plans New Giant Airplane in College Point to Span Atlantic", March 10, 1927.

7. ibid. "Aero Industry Revival Seen In College Point"

8. *Long Island Daily Press*, "Free Aviation Course May Be Given in Queens", October 14, 1929.

9. *Daily Star*, "Queens To Lose Aero Supply Corp.", November 29, 1930.

10. *Daily Star*, "Sikorsky Co. May Merge With United Aircraft", July 5, 1929.

11. *Daily Star*, "College Point Gives Lie to the Depression", March 30, 1932.

12. *Daily Star*, "Monsignor Schumack Dies in Rectory in College Point", December 29, 1920.

13. *North Shore Daily News*, "August Ebendick", August 25, 1932.

14. *North Shore Daily News*, "Rev. Arthur H. Halfmann Of College Point Is Dead", April 20, 1938.

15. *The Knickerbocker News*, "Former Coxsackie Minister Dies", April 17, 1940.

16. *Long Island Star Journal*, "Rev. Mottram Dies At 81", August 9, 1960.

17. *Memorial Day Exercises, Oscar Ammann Post No. 853*, 1928.

18. *Brooklyn Daily Standard Union*, "War Veteran Hangs Self After Divorce", October 4, 1922.

19. Military Service Record, New York State Archives.

20. *Daily Star*, "College Point Youth Dies As Submarine Grounds", March 18, 1920. The complete story of William Delamain's sad story was originally published in the Summer 2010 issue of *Landmark*, the Newsletter of the Poppenhusen Institute. It can also be accessed by visiting, http://www.pigboats.com/subs/h-boats.html.

21. Daily Star, "College Point Legionnaires Hear Story Of Heroic Death of Oscar Ammann in War", February 26, 1930.

Bibliography

Adler Julius Ochs. *History of the 306th Infantry*. 306th Infantry Association: 1935.

Aircraft Yearbook 1919, L.W.F. Engineering Company, Inc. Manufacturers Aircraft Association, New York City: 1919.

Andrews, James M. Col., *A Short History & Illustrated Roster of the 105th Infantry*. Edward Stern & Co., Philadelphia: 1917.

Baker, Leslie S., *The Story of Company B 106th Machine Gun Battalion 27th Division, U.S.A.* 1920.

Beamish, Richard J. and March, Francis A. Ph.D. *America's Part in the World War* The John C. Winston Company, Philadelphia, PA: 1919.

Binder, Frederick, M., and Reimers, David M., *All the Nations Under Heaven*: Columbia University Press, NY: 1995.

Boughton, V.T. *History of the Eleventh Engineers*. J.J. Little & Ives Company, New York, NY: 1927.

Brown, George Waldo & Pillsbury, Rosecrans W., *The American Army in the World War: A Divisional Record of the American Expeditionary Forces in Europe*. Overseas Book Company, Manchester, NH: 1921.

Chambers, Julius, *The Book of New York 1850-1912*. Book of New York Company New York: 1912.

Cochrane, Rexmond C., *Gas Warfare in World War I: The 29th Division in the Côtes de Meuse, October 1918*. U. S. Army Chemical Corps Historical Studies, Edgewood Arsenal, MD: 1959.

Coffman, Edward M., *The War to End All Wars*. University Press of Kentucky, 1998.

Crosby, Alfred W. *America's Forgotten Pandemic: The Influenza of 1918*. Cambridge University Press, Cambridge, England: 2003.

Cutchins, John A. *History of the Twenty-Ninth Division: Blue and Gray 1919.* Philadelphia: 1921.

Divisional Officers Designated by the Division Commander, *Official History of the 82nd Division American Expeditionary Forces 1917-1919.* Bobbs-Merrill Company, Indianapolis, IN: 1919.

Duffey, Ward E., Lieutenant. *The G. P. F. Book, Regimental History of the Three Hundred and Third Field Artillery*: 1921.

Duffy, Francis E., *Father Duffy's Story.* George H. Doran Company: 1919.

Eisenhower, John S.D. with Joanne Thompson Eisenhower. *Yanks: The Epic Story of the American Army in World War I.* New York: The Free Press, 2001.

Ewing, Joseph H., 29th Infantry Division: A Short History of a Fighting Division

Turner Publishing Company, Paducah, KY. 1922.

Ferrel, Robert H., *The Question of MacArthur's Reputation: Cote de Chaillon, October 14-16, 1918.* University of Missouri Press, Columbia, MO: 2008.

Gregory, Stephen. *Black Corona – Race and the Politics of Place In An Urban Community,* Princeton University Press, Princeton, NJ: 1998.

Harris, Stephen L. *Duty, Honor, Privilege: New York's Silk Stocking Regiment and the Breaking of the Hindenburg Line.* Brassey's Inc., Dulles, VA: 2001.

Haigh, Robert H. and Morris, David S., *The Killing Fields of World War One.* Sunflower University Press, Manhattan, KS: 1997.

Harris, Stephen L. *Duffy's War.* Washington, DC: Potomac Books, 2006.

Hendricks, Charles. *Combat and Construction: U.S. Army Engineers in World War I.* Fort Belvoir, Virginia: Office of History, U.S. Army Corps of Engineers: 1993.

Heller, Charles E., *Chemical Warfare in World War One: The American Experience 1917-1918.* Leavenworth Papers No. 10: 1984.

Hungerford, Edward. *With the Doughboys in France: A Few Chapters of an American Effort.* New York: The Macmillan Company, 1920.

Jacobson, Gerald F. *History of the 107th Infantry, U.S.A.* New York: Seventh Regiment Armory: 1920.

Keegan, John, *The First World War.* Alfred Knopf, 1999.

Krayer, Nicholas H. *History of Company E, 107th Infantry.* New York City: War Veterans' Association, NY: 1920.

March, Francis A. Ph. D. *History of the World War*. Philadelphia: United Publishers of the United States and Canada: 1919.

Miller, Nathan. *The U.S. Navy: A History*. New York: Quill, 1990.

Officers and Men of the 77th Division. *History of the 77th Division*. The 77th Division Association New York, Wynkoop Hallenbeck Crawford Company, New York: 1919.

O'Ryan, John F. *The Story of the 27th Division*. Wynkoop Hallenbeck Crawford Company, New York: 1921.

O'Shea, Stephen. *Back to the Front*. Avon Books, Inc.. New York, NY: 1996.

Perretti, Geoffrey. *America in the Twenties*. Simon and Schuster, New York: 1982.

Queens Borough: 1910-1920, Chamber of Commerce, Queens, NY: 1920.

Roberts, Michael D., *Dictionary of American Naval Squadrons, Volume 2*, Naval Historical Center, Washington DC: 2000.

Schuyler, Philip, V.R. Sergeant, *"C" Company 106th Machine Gun Battalion 27th Division, U.S.A.* Patterson Press, New York: 1919.

Seyfried, Vincent F., *Flushing in the Civil War Era 1837 to 1865*. 2001.

Skillman, Willis Rowland, *The A.E.F. Who They Were, What They Did, How They Did It* G.W. Jacobs, Philadelphia: 1920.

Society of the First Division, *History of the First Division During the World War 1917-1919*. John C. Winston Company, NY: 1922.

Stanley, Robert Henry, *The Movie Idiom: Film as a Popular Art Form* Waveland Press, Long Grove, IL: 2003

Summary of World War Work of the American YMCA, 1920.

Tiebout, Frank Bosworth, *A History of the 305th Infantry*. 305th Auxiliary, New York: 1919.

Thomas, Shipley. *History of the A.E.F.* George H. Doran Company, New York: 1920.

Tolzmann, Don Heinrich, *The German-American Experience*, Humanity Books, Amherst, NY: 2000.

Von Skal, George. *Illustrated History of the Borough of Queens*. F.T. Smiley Publishing Co. for the *Flushing Journal*, New York City: 1908.

Waller, Henry D., *History of the Town of Flushing*, J. H. Ridenour, Flushing: 1899.

Warner, Philip, *World War One: A Chronological Narrative.* Arms and Armor Press, London: 1995.

Williams, Paul Benjamin. *United States Lawn Tennis Association and the World War.* Robert Hamilton Co. New York: 1921.

Willis, Walter I., Ed. *Queens Borough, New York City 1910-1920.* Chamber of Commerce: 1920.

Yockelson, Mitchell A. *Borrowed Soldiers: Americans under British Command, 1918.* Norman:

University of Oklahoma Press, OK: 2008.

Zapotoczny, Walter S. *The Use of Poison Gas in World War I, and the Effect on Society.* 2007.

Websites

Adler, Julius Ochs. *History of the 306th Infantry.* 1935
http://www.longwood.k12.ny.us/history/upton/adler/adler.htm

Rouse, Nathan, *Grandpa's Diary*
http://e.wa/home.mindspring.com/wwdiary/

Second Battle of the Marne
http://www.worldwar1.com/dbc/2marne.htm

307th Infantry Memorial in Central Park
http://famousankles.com/

Eberhart, Dee R., *Illusions: World War II Poems*
http://www.sauruspress.com/travel/remembrance/ourq_river.htm

The Rainbow Division Monument
http://sites.communitylink.org/mac/PublicMemory.html

Embree Remembered
http://nuevoanden.com/embree/book.html

History of the Seventy-Seventh Division: The Baccarat Sector
http://www.longwood.k12.ny.us/history/upton/phase3.htm

History of the 316th Regiment of Infantry in the World War, 1918
http://www.archive.org/stream/historyof316thre00gloc/historyof316thre-00gloc_djvu.txt

World War One Popular Songs
http://www.besmark.com/ww1b.html
http://www.worldwar1.com/dbc/music.htm

The 10th and 20th Forestry Engineers of World War I
http://www.foresthistory.org/Research/WWI_ForestryEngineers.htm#service

Kerrick, Harrison S., *The Flag of the United States: Your Flag and Mine* Champlin Printing Company, Columbus, Ohio; 1925
http://www.crwflags.com/fotw/flags/us%5Esvc.html

A History of UCSF.
http://history.library.ucsf.edu/1899_affiliated_colleges.html

1st Battalion, 26th Infantry Regiment: "Blue Spaders"
https://www.globalsecurity.org/military/agency/army/1-26inf.htmWar

Service of the American Forestry Division
http://www.foresthistory.org/Research/WWI_ForestryEngineers.htm

Yanks in France: Western Front Jan. 1917 – Reserve
http://history.sandiego.edu/gen/ww1/yanks.html

The Influenza Pandemic of 1918.
http://www.ncbi.nlm.nih.gov/pmc/articles/PMC1446912/

A Typical Hospital Center. U.S. Army Medical Department
http://history.amedd.army.mil/booksdocs/wwi/adminamerexp/chapter22.html

U.S. Army Chemical Corps Museum
http://www.wood.army.mil/ccmuseum/ccmuseum/main.swf

Shipbuilding History – Sub-chasers
http://www.shipbuildinghistory.com